GW01186461

PRAISE FOR *UNICORNS OVER RAINBOWS*

'The author could have shared a huge amount of ideas
in a book five times the length. However as we see from
our glimpse into Mark's world during his darkest days, a
lack of ideas generally isn't the problem. The old adage
'less is more' applies here. With the right mindset, one
good small change is sometimes all you need. Nathan
Donaldson unpacks this simple yet powerful idea and
manages to entertain at the same time! A recommended
read for any leader curious about a different approach to
setting teams up for success.'

Ryan Clements, CIO, Queenstown Lakes District Council

'In the footsteps of *The One Minute Manager*, Nathan
Donaldson has written a parable for the budding
entrepreneur. On a one-hour plane trip, the reader
can absorb advice and lessons that may be the
difference between success and failure. Nathan is well
placed to write *Unicorns over Rainbows* as he has been
'entrepreneuring' for the last twenty years. As one of the
best-read CEOs I have ever met, he has fashioned the
latest thinking in this easy to absorb book. Buy, read, and
action it.'

David Parmenter, author of four business books including *Key
Performance Indicators*

'It took virtually no time at all for good, small changes to begin infiltrating the way we do things. Our culture was subtly but undoubtedly shifting. "Why not?" we'd say. "Let's just try it and see." Personally, as an over-thinker who wants all the answers before moving forward (and who previously mostly resisted change), Nathan's approach is game-changing.'

Christina Wedgwood, Owner/Founder of Intelligent Ink and Editor of *Unicorns over Rainbows*.

'*Unicorns Over Rainbows* is an absolute must-read for anyone seeking to truly revolutionize their workplace. With a perfect blend of engaging storytelling, practical advice, and actionable strategies, this book will ignite your imagination and equip you with the tools needed to create a workplace where productivity, collaboration, and happiness thrive. Whether you're a CEO, team leader, or aspiring entrepreneur, *Unicorns Over Rainbows* will inspire you to challenge conventional wisdom, embrace change, and unleash the true potential of your organization. Don't miss out on this game-changing book that will revolutionize the way you approach work and leadership.'

Tim Pointer, CEO, REASON & Rescue Metrics

UNICORNS OVER RAINBOWS

UNICORNS OVER RAINBOWS

*Make lasting, meaningful
change in your organization*

NATHAN DONALDSON

SWOOPING BAT

Unicorns Over Rainbows
nathandonaldson.com/unicornsoverrainbows
Copyright © Nathan Donaldson, 2023
All rights reserved.
ISBN 978-0-473-68479-2

CONTENTS

INTRODUCTION

I used to feel anxious when I browsed the business book section at the airport. I had read many books – the famous staples, the new, the fashionable. I had read them on short- and long-haul flights, and been excited by the idea that the lessons in such short books would have huge impacts. But not much had changed in my business or life.

Not that I didn't try. I had, and numerous times. I'd planned out the changes, got everything in place, and told the team what would happen. Nothing seemed to gain traction, though. Sometimes there was a short change of behavior, but inevitably, we would fall back to old ways, or worse. And each time I took a flight, and passed by the airport book store, I was reminded of this fact.

I have come to understand that there is a better way to make a change in my business, and this way will work for you too. I have seen substantial, revolutionary change by changing my mindset around change. It wasn't giant change management-led re-inventions that got us here. It was a series of small, incremental modifications that have taken us from an underperforming and chaotic business to the business we have today.

This is not meant to be a book with all the answers. Instead, it asks an important question: Could there be a better way to make and sustain change in a business or other organization?

This book also isn't about change management. When I looked around for help implementing ideas, I encountered the world of change management, and it scared me. Change management processes often looked more complex and intense than the ideas I was trying to put into place. Change management is a necessary and valuable tool to achieve significant, widespread change at a large scale, and it has its place. This book is instead about making change an incremental and sustainable practice, not a project.

Why listen to me? Great question! I have transformed my business, Boost, into one of the best workplaces in Australasia. We routinely win accolades for our workplace culture. We track happiness and productivity, and these are interdependent (happiness is the leading indicator of our productivity, and productivity creates happiness). Our first survey was in July 2016, and the team's happiness was 6.8/10. Through small incremental changes to our culture, we now sit between 9 and 9.6. Over the last three years, we have averaged 9.1/10, and have been recognized as one of the happiest IT companies in the world. You can see our current monthly score for happiness on our website (www.boost.co.nz/about-us)

That success has been made possible because of great ideas – many that are already out there, and that we're often desperate to make happen in our businesses. The trick is to introduce them with the right mindset and culture.

The Good Small Change model that this book introduces has been distilled from the behaviors and attitudes that have produced successful change in my business. Looking back over the last few years, we can identify over 40 small changes that we've implemented, as a team, that significantly changed how we do business. You can check out the list at **nathandonaldson. com/unicornsoverrainbows**

Ideas from John Cotter, Patrick Lencioni, Jim Collins, Peter Drucker, Carol Dweck, Brené Brown, and many others permeate our organization. These changes have transformed the business, the team, our clients, our families, and me.

This book is written in two parts. The first is a fable that introduces you to the key ideas through the story of business owner Mark as he discovers that he needs to improve his business. The second part elaborates on the model Mark uncovers in the fable – a model for incremental, sustainable change that I call the Good Small Change model.

This book isn't a how-to guide to improve your business. I have purposefully shied away from giving specific practices or advice, or even explaining what Mark's business does. I hope you can look beyond *what* Mark does in the book to *how* Mark does things. To be more precise, how Mark changes his mindset to enable and empower change.

After reading this book, I hope you will apply the Good Small Change model in your organization. I believe that you will see the success that I've seen, that your team will be excited to hear and implement your new ideas and that you will get the swooping bat on your homepage that I have always dreamed of.

PART I: THE FABLE

THE PHONE CALL

Mark had just got home when his phone rang. It was Rick, the company's biggest customer.

It wasn't unusual for him to call, but it didn't happen often. The contract with Rick accounted for most of the company's revenue – not an ideal situation to be in, with so much relying on one customer. But the relationship was strong, and they had been working together for over six years. Mark picked up the call.

"Hi Mark, how are things? Listen, I've got a bit of bad news," started Rick. "You remember how we were acquired last year? Our new IT department has struggled to finish the company-wide computer upgrade, and they have decided to use our budget for next year." He paused. "Beginning next month, we'll be cutting down to 20 percent of our usual monthly order. I am talking to everyone in the organization to try and find some more money, but I'm not sure what I can do. I'll get in touch next week with an update. Sorry to spring this on you, but I wanted to let you know as soon as I could."

Mark felt sick to his stomach. He thanked Rick for the call, hung up, and stood, unsure of what to do. More than half of the business's monthly income – and the work for a half-dozen people – now gone. He had to make some sales, and quickly.

THE NEXT MORNING

The drive to work was a blur. An hour on the highway in the rain, crawling through the traffic, his windscreen wipers keeping time. Mark wanted this day to be over and yet it had barely begun.

In the week since Rick's call, Mark had poured endless hours into spreadsheets with his CFO Amy; they'd calculated and re-calculated their position, and tried to find more money. But he'd quickly realized that there was no other option. They had to cut costs.

As he arrived at the office and greeted his team, he cast his mind back to the time before Rick's call. The business had never been in better shape. Finances were strong, even with so much relying on just one customer; they'd enjoyed another month of steady growth, and the team were comfortable with how they were doing things. Two months prior they'd been confident enough to delete a whole product line that was difficult and time-consuming to support. Mark and the team had been sure it was the right thing to do, and Rick's orders had filled the gap. The future had looked rosy!

But today, Mark was making five people redundant. One by one, Mark called some of his team into the office, each time explaining the situation and what he had to do. He was sorry to have to say goodbye to them.

Naomi was the last of the five. She wanted to stay and help. Mark and Naomi agreed she would work one day a week until the business was back on its feet, and Mark was grateful that she would be there when they – hopefully – sprung back. Mark followed her out of his office and into the main work area.

"Hey everyone, could I have your attention for a few minutes?" Mark looked around as people stopped working and talking and turned to face him. He took a deep breath.

"I got a call from Rick last week. The business that acquired his company is putting his projects on hold so that they can redirect the money to the urgent IT needs of the wider organization. What this means for us is that Rick's order going ahead will be only a fraction of what it usually is. We don't know when – or if – this will increase, or by how much."

The team sat silently. Someone coughed. Mark looked around. There were many worried faces. This wasn't getting any easier.

"I've had to act quickly. This morning I talked to Jim, Graham, Tina, Lionel, and Naomi. They have all accepted redundancy and will leave today to start looking for new roles. Naomi will stay on one day a week for now. I am working with them all to find something suitable and will be introducing them to some great people in my wider network."

He took a moment to take in the team's faces. "Does anyone have any questions?"

There were many questions.

REPORTING TO 'THE BOARD'

Mark stayed at the office for an extra hour. He often did, as it gave the traffic a chance to clear. But tonight was different – he was also anxious about the conversation he would have with his 'Board of Directors.' This is how Mark thought of his wife Patricia and young son Luke; they were the people he felt he was held to account by most of all.

Patricia needed to know the implications now that Mark had assessed the accounts with Amy and made part of his team redundant. They had talked about Rick's news, but that had been a conversation about putting out the fire – not fire-proofing the house.

Mark ran through the conversation in his head as he hit the highway once again, re-thinking the numbers, the possibilities, the best- and worst-case scenarios. It was not a pretty picture, even with four-and-a-half fewer salaries.

Luke ran unsteadily to the door as Mark walked into the house. Mark scooped him up for a hug and carried him upstairs. It was good to be home. Patricia was at the table working on her PhD. Mark made them both a hot drink, and they sat down to chat about the day.

"How did it go?" Patricia asked.

"Better than I could have hoped, and still the worst thing I've ever done," Mark replied. "Everyone was gracious and supportive, but it was hard telling the team what was happening. There were many questions and people were naturally feeling uneasy about the future." Mark paused. "I didn't have a lot of answers today, Patty."

With Luke tucked up in bed, Patricia and Mark sat down at the kitchen table. Mark pulled up a spreadsheet on his laptop. "Here's the situation. Best-case scenario, we're going to need to find $100,000 dollars to put into the business, and soon. That is, if we can't make sales to cover what Rick would have ordered. Worst-case scenario, well... The worst-case scenario is we have to make some very difficult decisions..." Mark trailed off.

They had moved out of town to a small beachside community a few years ago, before Luke was born. It was their first family home. It had been a good trade-off: A bit more of a commute, but a house by the ocean. It was their dream home, where they had started their family, and now they could see that they might have to sell to keep the business afloat. Patty put her arm around Mark's shoulders: "It's only a house."

Mark nodded, unable to say anything.

MAKING A PLAN

Mark hadn't slept well, but the next morning he was energized, and his head was clear. Today he would make a plan, and he would fix this. He had a list:

One: Make calls, set meetings, and start meeting potential clients. Get the business pipeline filled up again.

Two: Find some other new ideas to make the business better.

Three: Rally the troops.

When Mark had started the business 13 years ago, everything had come quite easily. There were a few months at the start where he was calling and meeting as many businesses as possible. Building relationships and beating the bushes for sales. After that, the sales seemed to just start coming. The business had started as two people, grown to five, then a dozen, then 25, with no real signs of slowing. They'd grown a reliable team organically, and there was always enough money to make payroll, and set aside some more for a rainy day. Not a big business, but a good business. Or so Mark thought. The call from Rick had shaken him.

First on Mark's list today was hustling. Getting out there. Visiting old customers and finding new ones. He sat at his desk, opened his contact list, and started sorting through who he could contact.

Mark poked his head out of his office, and got the attention of Ryan, his personal assistant. "Ryan, I think I'm going to need some help. I need to be out of the office meeting potential new customers. It's going to take a lot of back and forth to get it working well. Would you be able to manage my calendar?"

"Sure" Ryan grinned, "I can do that, no problem! How's this going to work?"

Mark was excited by Ryan's enthusiasm; he was helpful to a fault. "I'll make initial contact with the potential customer, and once they agree to a catch-up, I will pass them on to you. You work out where and when and put it in my calendar." Mark watched as he made a few notes and nodded.

"I'm on it!" Ryan said.

Mark was now satisfied that his first task was under control. He closed his contact list and turned to the second item on his list: Making the business better. He thought about his business friends and what had happened to them when they went through tough times. A couple of years ago, Carol, a business friend in town, had to cut costs, downsize, and rebuild her company's pipeline of work when the economy slumped. He was pretty sure she'd recommended a book that had helped her through the downturn. He rummaged through the bookcase by his desk until he found a slim book with a bright yellow cover. Would it contain the silver bullet he was looking for? Did this have the answer? Part of the answer? He certainly hoped so. He got Ryan's attention again.

"Ryan, could you hold my calls for the rest of the day? I've got something that needs my attention right away."

Ryan looked up, "Of course, no problem. Need a coffee while you work?"

"Yes, thanks."

Ryan delivered a mug to Mark's desk and closed the door behind him. Mark opened up the book, and began to read.

The book was good. It was assured and loaded with inspiring language. It was full of ideas: Improve alignment, get cash faster, pay bills slower, get the right people on the bus, make sure they were in the right seat, march them to the South Pole, make sure they use dogs and not horses, make them go fast but not too fast, travel the same amount every day, don't die, don't get lost, have a purpose, have a vision, chant your values, sing a song, be unique, don't grow broke, know your clients, know your team, fire some bullets, have some cannons, make a snowball, spin up the flywheel, cut costs, put up prices, and be audacious.

Mark's head was swimming. He looked around the office to discover everyone else had gone home – and switched off the lights behind them, leaving him in his little island of office light. It had become dark outside too. Mark sighed. At least the traffic would be light on the way home. He got up, tapped the Yoda bobble head on his desk for good luck, and left the empty, quiet office.

On the highway, Mark started to sift through the ideas from the book he had just read. It all made sense. If he could implement the book's suggestions, he was sure he would have a stronger, more resilient business. Maybe he could save the business after all.

Luke was already in bed when Mark got home. Patricia was sitting in the lounge working on her laptop. She looked up with a smile. As soon as his satchel had hit the table, Mark started to tell her about the book he had read. He was excited to share, and keen for Patricia to be just as excited about the dogs and the cannons and the flywheels. Then he realized he had been talking for 10 minutes and had barely taken a breath. "Patty, what do you think?" Mark asked, excited like a puppy with a new bone.

Patricia took a deep breath. "That all sounds great... I mean really great. I'm not sure I caught it all though. It sounds like a lot of work, and a lot of change."

Mark agreed, "Yes, yes doesn't it? I can't wait to get started!"

EVERYONE GETS A BOOK

The next morning, Mark waited for his management team in the conference room. He'd decided to surprise each member of his management team with a copy of the book.

Slowly the leadership team filed into the room. He greeted each of them in turn.

First in was Amy, his CFO, who came in with a stack of spreadsheets under her arm. She'd started as his PA a long time ago, and was naturally kind and intelligent – but she proved herself excellent with finances and quickly moved into her current role. In fact, Mark wondered if money was the thing she took most seriously in the world. It seemed that no matter what they talked about in the office, it always came back to the company's finances.

Next in was Tyler, the Business Development Manager. He had a takeaway coffee in one hand, and was using the thumb of the other to swipe right on his phone every second or so. Tyler was an old college friend of Mark, and while they were both in their early 40s, Tyler never really seemed to have left the dorm. Not that anyone ever held that against him.

Carlos sauntered in behind Tyler, looking slightly worse for wear. He spotted Mark and perked up his face, giving a thumbs up as if to say, "Yep, all good, boss." Carlos had long been a cheerleader for Mark and the business – always there, always positive. It made him ideal as Head of Product, as he was passionate about improving the value for customers.

Finally, Jane wandered in looking relaxed and somewhat

mystified as to why they were meeting. She'd bounced from role to role since she started, before finally making her way to COO because Mark thought – well, hoped – she'd apply herself best there.

Mark sighed inwardly. It wasn't that they were a bad team. But he couldn't quite shift the feeling that they reflected his performance. It was a sobering thought.

Everyone chatted as they took their seats. As they started to quieten down, Mark made his announcement. "Great news everyone. I know the past few days have been stressful, and I have been working hard on coming up with a plan. I want to share it with you and get your feedback."

The team stole glances at each other. Carlos spoke up.

"It's not the bat again, is it?"

A few years prior, Mark had wanted to change the company homepage to show a giant bat swooping out of the darkness to snare a fish from a pond. He hadn't been able to explain why he thought it was a good idea, he really just liked that it was bold, striking, and different. No one – literally no one – except Mark thought it was a great idea. It had become a recurring joke in the office, a shorthand for an irrelevant and poorly-thought-out idea. Mark still liked it and secretly believed they might still have a bat on the homepage one day. He had noticed, though, that even he was getting less excited about the idea as time passed.

"Oh, not that – despite how amazing it would have been." He handed out books as he spoke. "This book, though, will change how we do business and get us back up to speed! I stopped by the book shop this morning especially. I believe if we adopt the models in here—" he held it up with one hand and slapped it with the other "—then we will be a healthier, stronger business. I want you to read this book this week, and then we can assign tasks for the implementation."

He continued: "My plan for today is to work out what we

need to do now to build back our sales to cover the shortfall in the coming months. We need to get busy, people." Mark was on a roll. He knew that if he wanted more from his team, he had to lead the way. "My plan is to make meetings and beat the streets. I have been through my contact list and have 180 existing or previous clients and contacts. I have a goal of 30 meetings a week. We will make more sales!"

The team around the table looked anxious and confused. Mark had hoped this enthusiasm would rally the troops. He was convinced that this shiny, easy-to-read morsel would have everything that the team needed to overhaul operations and get back on track. He felt like he had done most of the work for them: He had found the book, read the book, decided it was important, and then bought them each a copy. *It couldn't be easier, or more important,* thought Mark. They'd be sure to love it.

Amy slid the book into her bag with her notebook. Jane scanned the back cover absently. Tyler stared out the window at the pub across the road. Carlos nodded. Mark was hopeful, but unsure why Carlos was nodding; he must be ready to get going.

BOOK? WHAT BOOK?

Two weeks had passed since Mark handed out the book. During that time, he'd frantically hit his goal of 30 meetings each week – and had a word with Ryan about booking back-to-back meetings at opposite ends of town with no breathing space. Even so, Mark thought the efforts were worthwhile. He was on a good path.

Now he was going over the notes for the afternoon's leadership meeting. Having re-read the book twice more in the intervening days, Mark was excited to hear his team's enthusiasm and collective ideas. He was sure they would have an extra spring in their step as they walked into the room.

Mark and Ryan had prepared the room for the meeting. Mark had the agenda on the whiteboard and Post-its and Sharpies at each seat, while Ryan had put together a platter of everyone's favorite snacks.

Mark was a bundle of nervous energy. But as the team began to arrive for the meeting, he didn't see the excitement he had expected.

"Let's go around the table and each of us will share our favorite chapter, followed by why and how we will implement it in our daily work. Who wants to start?" asked Mark. He looked around the room. The team was fidgeting and appeared to be busy taking notes and organizing stationery on the table in front of them. The silence dragged out.

"Carlos, what was your favorite chapter?" Mark nodded encouragingly.

Carlos stuttered, "I only read the introduction, but that was good. I feel like maybe that's all you need to read. You know…"

Mark didn't know. Carlos paused as he realized Mark wanted him to continue.

"You know, business books… they tell you everything in the intro and then just pad out the rest of the book. Am I right?" Carlos looked around.

For some reason, there were enthusiastic nods from around the table.

"So, I think the bit I liked the best was the special bus seats. I'm not sure how those relate to what we do, though. Maybe that is in one of the later chapters!" Carlos exclaimed like he had solved world peace. He leaned back in his chair with the expression of someone who hadn't done his homework but somehow nailed the presentation regardless.

Mark frowned. "Thanks, Carlos." He wasn't sure how to be positive about Carlos's contribution to the discussion. He forced a broad smile. "Amy, what was your favorite part?"

"I didn't read it," Amy said in her customary direct way. "I didn't think it was that important."

Mark tried not to show his disappointment. "You mean you didn't finish the book?" he asked hopefully.

"No, I didn't start it," Amy clarified. She stared at Mark.

"Has anyone read the book?"

His management team sat silently.

"A part of the book?"

Still nothing.

Mark pushed for something. Tyler said he wasn't sure how the book was supposed to actually help them. He hadn't started it, but had become confused when he looked at the back cover. He couldn't understand how it was meant to help sales. It seemed to be about everything but.

Jane was frozen, wide-eyed with a cracker in her mouth, like a deer caught in headlights. Slowly she started to chew. Mark watched, waiting to hear from her once she finished.

The room was filled with the sound of Jane trying desperately to chew the cracker without finishing it. Mark looked away. Jane let out a sigh of relief and Mark snapped his head back to see her mouth full of cracker once again. *How did she do that,* thought Mark. *I only looked away for a second. I suppose that's why she runs Operations. If only we were a fill-your-mouth-with-crackers company,* Mark lamented to himself.

"OK, great. Great. Yes, well, we... we have the agenda... but..." Mark was lost. He turned to face the whiteboard – to hide his face for a moment while he tried to compose himself and push down the frustration that was bubbling up from deep inside him.

He took deep breaths and picked up a whiteboard marker to make it look like he had a direction. While he removed and replaced the cap a few times, he told himself that this was just a small setback, and that all he had to do was find a way to make them read the book. Well, not *make* them, but encourage them. Vigorously. A competition? Paying them to read it? Wasn't he already doing that? Surely they can do this one simple thing for him – for the company. He could read it aloud to them... But that felt a bit extreme, a bit too elementary school. Was there anything in the book that could help him figure out how to get his team to read the book? Something between the South Pole and the snowballs and the songs?

Amy spoke up from behind him. "Mark, I think we are just too busy to read the book. Why don't you just tell us what to do? We want to help, but we aren't used to this sort of stuff like you are. It's... new."

Amy said "new." Mark suspected she meant "a distraction."

Mark swallowed hard, and apologized to the team for not doing a great job of introducing the book. They went around the room a few times gathering ideas on how to encourage themselves, and each other, to read the book, before Mark called the meeting to a close. He was still not confident he had his team on board.

A LITTLE BIT OF LIGHT

Mark and Patricia sat at the kitchen table after dinner. "How did the team find your new book?" she asked.

Mark sighed. "Well, Carlos appears to have read the back cover. Amy point blank said she didn't have time to read it, and the rest were somewhere in between – if that's even possible."

Mark's phone rang. He glanced at the screen and turned it to show Patricia. It was Rick, again.

"Hey Rick, how's it going?" Mark tried to hide the fear in his voice.

"Sorry to ring this late, Mark, I just wanted to let you know as soon as possible. I have a small piece of good news."

Mark held his breath. He needed something good.

Rick continued. "I have been working with the head of our department, and we have found some more money. We would like to increase our order for next month. Not back up to our usual levels, but we think we can get back to around 50 percent."

Mark was nodding and giving Patricia an enthusiastic thumbs up. "That's great news Rick! I appreciate the work you're doing to get back to where we were. It makes a huge difference for us. How about I get Tyler to call you in the morning to confirm the details?"

They said their goodbyes, agreeing to catch-up the following week. Mark plopped himself back in his chair. "Well, that's certainly going to help! "

He was glad. But the Rick situation had brought something stark to light: He'd grown too dependent on one good client over the years – and their sales function clearly wasn't working well enough to keep them afloat. They'd spent a long time unchallenged. Now their lack of stability was clear.

Right now, though, Mark had a bit of breathing room. For the first time in a fortnight, he smiled.

A NEW START

Rick's good news had put a spring in Mark's step. It wasn't enough to put things back where they were, but enough that Mark could breathe a bit more.

The next day, as Mark updated the customer relationship management software with notes from his twentieth customer meeting of the week, he had his next great idea. It was right in front of him: The potentially incredible – and definitely expensive – CRM.

The team had installed the CRM a year ago with the intention of making more sales. Mark had felt sure at the time that a new customer relationship management tool was precisely what they needed to understand their customer needs, send out quotes, and generally put all their customer knowledge in one place. Instead, it quickly became a glorified Rolodex – if your Rolodex was a drawer full of business cards and the odd scrap of paper with a preferred coffee order or a child's birthdate on it.

Mark's stroke of genius was that the team should start using the CRM to its fullest potential. His new plan was to turn the CRM into a sales-making, deal-closing, lead-generating machine. This would be the start of a new era of productivity and profit!

He spent the morning mapping out a full sales and customer interaction procedure, and a series of flow charts for each department across the business. A fully realized, fully utilized CRM would be the one source of truth about all contacts, customers, and deals. It was a work of art.

Mark knew the management team was still struggling to read the book, but he figured they would be so excited about the new processes that they would be keen to tackle both at once. This CRM was going to be a winner.

This time, he would avoid the mistakes he'd made when he'd introduced the book. This time, he would take each of his department heads through the processes separately. They would understand what needed to be done and how. Hadn't Amy suggested at that last meeting that he just tell them what to do? Well, the success of the project would be measured by how many new sales they made each month. There was no way this could fail.

He headed straight to Tyler's office. "Tyler, good morning! Guess what? I got another call from Rick last night."

Tyler was smiling, but still looked anxious. "Oh yeah, good news, I hope?"

"Great news! By next month we'll be up to about 50 percent of his previous monthly spend!"

Tyler smiled. "That is great news!" Then he frowned. "But doesn't that still leave us a bit short?"

"Well, yes, we still have some work to do, that is for sure," said Mark. "But this gives us some time to make real changes to the business that improve our situation." Mark beamed.

"Changes? Did you have something in mind?"

This was just the invitation Mark had been looking for. Before Tyler could blink, Mark had his laptop open on Tyler's desk and was showing him an impressive web of interlinked flowcharts.

"As you can see," he started, "all the sales processes are in blue. If it's an existing client, you'll start with this rectangle." He tapped the screen. "But a new client you'd start with this triangle. It mostly just flows right-to-left, and it shows you where you'll need to refer to another chart. Orange for internal, green for external, and yellow for... oh, yes, yellow for a bit of both. It's all in the key down the bottom."

Tyler looked at the screen. It looked like a preschooler had eaten a box of crayons before throwing up on a wall.

"Don't worry, Tyler. I'll have Ryan print and laminate this for you. Then you can refer to it as you do your work."

Tyler made enthusiastic noises, nodded vigorously, and thanked Mark.

"This is going to be great," Tyler said. "I think. I mean why wouldn't it?" Tyler's phone rang. "I'd better get this; could be our next big sale." Tyler gave Mark a big thumbs up as he answered the phone.

ROUND TWO

The leadership team was once again assembled in the boardroom. Mark made sure to thank everyone for their hard work before revealing the good news.

"Last night, I got a call from Rick, and he's increasing his monthly order – not back to the previous level, but it will certainly help.

"Now, as you all know, I have been working on a new process to make our sales efforts more efficient and successful. It doesn't involve any new tools, just using the ones we already have more effectively. The key tool we have for sales is our CRM. If we make better use of this tool, we can make real gains in our sales."

Amy looked confused. "What is a CRM? Is that the really expensive software we pay for each month? I thought that tracked inventory?"

"No, you're thinking of our ERP system," Jane corrected.

"Well, it's expensive, so we should use it more." Amy crossed her arms.

"The ERP manages the operations side of the business," explained Mark. "Our CRM is to manage our clients. We can use it better, and we will make more sales – I just need your help."

The team perked up. He continued.

"Once we know more about our people – and load that information into the CRM – we'll be able to see what kinds of problems they're facing. So, this is your chance to learn about our customers and then figure out where we can change things up for everyone and make things better for them. This is going to be big, and if we're all on board, then it will fix everything. How does that sound?"

He pulled out his large, laminated flowcharts from behind the whiteboard. "The key is to capture as much information about our clients as possible, and to use that information to provide better service to them. We also need to have all of our deals in the pipeline tool within the CRM and update them every day..."

FLOWERS FOR PATRICIA

When Mark arrived home that night, it wasn't until he closed the door behind him that he remembered he had intended to get Patricia flowers. Failing as CEO, and failing as a husband. It was all starting to feel quite hard.

"How was your day?" he asked .

"Great day today – I got another chapter finished and took Luke for a walk on the beach. How did your day go?"

"Well, I thought it was good. But the more I think about it, the more worried I'm getting. I've come up with a great idea. I think I have Carlos and Tyler on board. But I'm not sure about the others. I think I'll have to provide some more support and see how we get on." Mark paused. "I *hope* Carlos and Tyler are on board."

"Well, if there is anything I can do, let me know." Patricia smiled at Mark. "By the way, John called – he asked if you'd like a game of chess at his place soon."

"Great idea," said Mark. "A game of chess might be just what I need to get my mind off work for a bit."

THINGS GET WORSE AT WORK

The next week, while distracted by thinking about how the team were committing to his new processes, Mark nearly knocked Ryan over as he strode into the office.

"Shoot, sorry Ry!" Mark looked up. Ryan had a folder in his hands.

"Got this for you, boss. Thought you might like to see how we are doing with the CRM."

Mark took the folder from Ryan, wondering if it was good news or bad.

"How about a coffee to get you started on that?" Ryan asked.

"Is the folder good news? No, don't answer. Yes, a coffee would be great. I'll be in my office."

Mark waited for the coffee, not willing to take the risk of bad news while uncaffeinated. Ryan placed the coffee on his desk and beat a hasty retreat.

Mark opened the plain brown folder and started to read the first sheet of paper, taking sips of coffee with each sentence. Ryan had done a good job of the report; it was clear and concise. However, that wasn't that difficult, given there was little to report on. Tyler and Jane hadn't logged in all week. Carlos had shuffled some contacts into different lists. The only one who had been using the CRM consistently was Amy, who had looked at the pipeline and sales projections multiple times a day.

Mark's coffee was already empty. He caught Ryan's eye and mimed drinking from a mug. Ryan nodded and headed for the kitchen. This was going to be a long day.

Mark began to sort through the situation in his head. He had told the team what they needed to do; he had given them clear instructions. He had even designed the process for them. He'd invited them to think about how they could transform things for their clients. He had set clear expectations. The flow charts were detailed! He had surely done everything that was expected of a leader? This was the easy stuff – the low-hanging fruit. Mark wondered how he was going to fix this. Why hadn't they followed through?

Never one to let ignorance stand in the way of action, Mark sent a message to Ryan: *Schedule a meeting for the leadership team ASAP*. Shortly followed by another: *Thanks*.

ACCUSATIONS

"So, no one is using the CRM. What's going on?"

There was silence across the room. It had taken until the end of the day to get the team into the room, and one or two of them had packed their bags and were already eyeing the exit. Mark was unable to hide the frustration in his voice.

"Tyler. What was stopping you from using the CRM?"

"Yeah, well, I was out of the office meeting people and then I had to send Paul a quote. He wanted it quickly, so I sent it through in an email. I figured that was the best thing to do. Ahh, then, I *was* going to put it in the CRM, but Paul went quiet." Tyler also went quiet.

"So, we have a quote out with Paul, but it's not in our pipeline?" Mark felt his teeth clenching.

"Yeah, but he wanted it right away, so I thought it was good to get it to him quickly. Surely that's the right thing?"

Mark turned to Carlos, "How about you? Did you follow our new process with the CRM this week?"

Carlos had used the CRM and looked pretty pleased with himself. "Yes, I did. I made some new lists and moved customers on to them so that we had them categorized."

Mark had already checked Carlos's efforts. "I did see the new lists," he said. "Could you share what they are for and how you named them with the team?"

"I made three lists: Customers I like working with; customers who pay well; and everyone else." It was clear Carlos hadn't said this out loud yet, and he started to lose momentum. "I named them *Legends*, *Piggy Banks*, and *Losers*."

The room remained silent. He added: "I couldn't think of a name for the *Piggy Banks* that started with L."

"Leprechauns!" blurted out Jane. The group looked confused. "Because they have a pot of gold," she added.

Mark looked around. "So, am I right in thinking that, in summary, the only use the CRM had this week was for failed alliteration?"

Tyler spoke up. "I think we all wanted to use it more – to make things better. But it's a lot to change all at once, and especially while we're already busy."

He waited for someone else to say something.

Amy spoke up. "Our pipeline is empty, and I'm worried about cashflow. We need more sales. I look every day, but nothing ever changes." She added, "In our CRM."

Yes, nothing ever changes, thought Mark.

"Can we head home? I'm really tired." Jane was standing and gathering her belongings. "Can we talk about this tomorrow?"

Mark's shoulders slumped. "Sure, everyone head home. Let's look at this again tomorrow."

CHESS WITH JOHN

John was their next-door neighbor. Well, not next door; he lived on the hill above the beach. When Mark and Patricia had moved into their dream house a few years earlier, John was the first person they met.

Mark remembered the day well. They'd only been there a week, and there'd been a knock at the door while they were unpacking. Baxter, their three-year-old Schnauzer, started barking like a loon. Mark was downstairs sorting out Luke's room, so he yelled out, "I'll get it" to Patricia.

He opened the front door to a tall and lean older man in a straw fedora and a two-piece tan suit. The man introduced himself with a distinct English accent.

"Hullo, I'm John. I used to walk the previous owners' dog. I was walking past and noticed that you had a dog too."

Baxter had a habit of barking at passersby, and had found a spot on the patio from which to make his presence known. The whole neighborhood must have heard Baxter by now.

"I live up the hill, in that yellow house there." John gestured.

Mark wondered where this was going.

"Would you mind if I popped in a few times a week to walk your dog?" John asked.

Mark was taken aback – not because a stranger would walk a dog, but because a stranger *wanted* to *walk* this dog.

"Well, that would be fantastic. The vet has said Baxter is borderline psychotic, and he struggles to get on with other dogs." Mark felt like he needed to set expectations here. Baxter wasn't the most well-behaved dog in the world, and he had been barking the whole time Mark and John had been talking.

John laughed. "Sounds like we will get on like a house on fire!"

Mark wasn't sure what that meant, but he hated walking the dog. And if John was only borderline psychotic, this might work out OK.

As it turned out, John was far from psychotic – and that suited Mark perfectly. Over the years, John had turned out to be more than a neighbor, dog walker and chess player. He was also an accomplished business leader who had consulted for organizations big and small all over the world. Their conversations about business and their respective experiences kept Mark enthralled. John was always asking Mark insightful questions that had an annoying way of getting quickly to the nub of the issues. Mark hoped that tonight John would have something wise to say.

It was eight in the evening by the time he knocked on John's door.

"Mark! Come in, I've got wild boar bacon for sandwiches." John beamed, motioning for Mark to come inside.

John's enthusiasm was contagious. There was no way for the weight of the world to sit on your shoulders while John was forcing the world's best bacon sandwiches – and a world-class red wine – on you.

The chessboard was already set up by the time they sat down. Mark was playing white. They leapt into the game, Mark leading and John responding. It didn't take too long before John's superior strategy and tactics began to undo Mark's momentum.

"Mate in four," said John.

"What, really?" Mark had thought the game might go a little longer and that he might be able to mount something of a counterattack. But when John said "Mate in four," it was inevitably mate in four.

John pointed at his knight. "You relied too much on your bishop, so once this takes him and puts you in check, you are done for."

Now Mark could see it. He reached across and shook John's hand.

"Another?" said John as he began to rearrange the pieces into their starting positions.

"Actually, I was wondering if you could give me some advice with a problem I am having at work," Mark asked, feeling slightly nervous.

"Well, this sounds intriguing." John took a quick trip to the kitchen and returned with more sandwiches and the wine bottle. "Freshen your glass? Now tell me, what can I help you with?" he asked while he topped up Mark's drink.

"Well, there are two or three things. But I'm not sure what is most important. Can I tell you about the last few weeks?"

Mark took John through the ups and downs with Rick, and his attempts to make some longer-term changes with the leadership team. He explained how he'd shared the book – but how no one seemed interested in reading it, let alone transforming their operations based on the teachings within. Mark talked about his efforts to get the CRM working harder; he explained how the team seemed invested, and the great engagement at the start – but how they didn't commit to it in any meaningful way that would have got results. As Mark went on, he felt himself become more despairing and frustrated.

"And that's where we are at."

Mark sat back in his chair. John took a moment.

"That's a lot. Are you doing OK?"

"I think I'm a bit frustrated. I am trying to improve the business, but the team doesn't seem to be on my side." Mark swallowed. "I don't think I'm a very effective leader."

That was hard to say out loud.

"Why do you say that?" John was looking relaxed. Mark took a moment to reply.

"If I was a good leader, the team would pick up my ideas and run with them. They would fully commit, and they would be excited to try new things."

John smiled broadly. "Why?"

"Why would they pick up my ideas and be excited?"

John nodded.

"Because they can see they are good ideas," continued Mark.

"Are they good ideas?" asked John.

"Well, yes. I think so. I mean, they aren't bad ideas. I think."

"Let's assume they are great ideas, the best ideas. Why might your team not be jumping to implement them?" questioned John.

Mark was lost for a moment. "I don't know."

"Hmm. Another game?" John didn't elaborate.

Mark headed home after two more games, both of which he lost. Patricia was already in bed by the time he got in.

"Good game?" she mumbled.

"I lost three games, but I think I might get a win next time," said Mark. He didn't think he would win next time, but it was good to be positive. He sure had a lot to think about.

BACK TO THE FLYWHEEL

The next day, Mark was pondering his conversation with John on the drive to work. If the problem wasn't whether his ideas were good or not, what *was* the problem? What was he trying to achieve with the flow charts and the processes?

By the time Mark had pulled into his carpark he had started to formulate a plan.

Mark's new – and as-yet untested – assumption was that the tools and processes he had introduced to the team last week were too complex and convoluted. On top of that they were too prescriptive. He couldn't treat the team like mindless automatons relentlessly repeating tasks with endless precision. They needed to be invested in the changes they were making – and feel like they could actually make some changes without things going wrong. As Tyler had said, it had been a lot to change all at once.

At his desk, Mark doodled. What was at the heart of the idea he had presented last week? Could he identify one thing that he wanted the team to do? Could he identify how that one thing would help? Apart from the aimless doodle, his pad was blank. He was starting to realize that simpler wouldn't necessarily mean easier – at least, not for him.

He stared at the paper, and the paper stared back at him, daring him to try and make sense of the undiscovered Kandinsky that was the CRM process.

Mark started a fresh page, and boldly scrawled *CONNECTION* in the middle of the page, then put a box around it with a flourish. This was what the CRM project was about! Around the outside, he wrote *Customers*, *Departments*, *Team Members* and *Business*. Each word got boxed and connected to the middle box by a line with arrows at each end. Above each line he wrote *INFORMATION*.

Now he was starting to get somewhere. He started to add different pieces of information to each of the boxes. For *Customers* he wrote *Contact Details*, *Personal Information*, *Previous Deals* and *New Deals*. For *Business* he wrote *Pipeline*, *Deals Won* and *Deals Lost*. In the box for *Team Members*, he wrote *Customers* and *Deals*. It was starting to look like a tattooed alien octopus.

This was still feeling a bit complicated. Mark tapped the paper with his pen. Success was the result of having the right information at the right time to best help the team, the customer, and the business. Aha! That was it! Mark picked up his pen and wrote six words on the page.

"Ry, can you get the team together? Thanks!"

THE BIG REVEAL

Mark took a deep breath. Looking around the room, he could see that half the team had checked out before they had even walked in. Jane was idly stirring her coffee with a wooden stick. Amy clearly was thinking about spreadsheets. Tyler laughed at his phone and typed a message to someone. Carlos looked cautiously enthusiastic, and tired.

Mark was going to have to do something to get their attention if he had any chance of getting them onboard.

"I'm sorry. The way I approached the CRM stuff last week was terrible. I can do better." Mark looked around again. There was a lot of nodding. He hadn't expected quite that much nodding. He struggled to remember where he was heading. "I've had a think."

The team stiffened in their seats.

"I have simplified the CRM process so that we can experience the benefits more easily."

Jane cleared her throat. Mark was excited at the idea of getting some engagement from the team.

"Jane, you've got a question?"

Jane spluttered. "Coffee... gone down the wrong way..." She recovered, looked around the room, and gave Mark a big thumbs up.

"Thanks Jane." Mark frowned and turned back to the team.

Carlos turned and whispered to Amy. "It'll be the bat again!" They both sniggered. Mark didn't know that this running joke had kept Carlos and Amy entertained for years. Once, Carlos doodled Mark as a bat. A paunchy, middle-aged bat, sitting in front of a computer, staring at a spreadsheet. He'd slipped it to Amy as he walked past her desk, and she'd kept it folded in the bottom of her desk drawer since, just out of sight.

"It's not the bat!" Mark exclaimed. Mark was staring at Carlos.

"Right, got it, not the bat," Carlos muttered.

Mark went to the whiteboard and wrote RIGHT INFO, RIGHT TIME, RIGHT NOW. He underlined it twice, for emphasis.

Mark turned back to the team. "Those six words are what it's about. We need better information to make better decisions. We all need access to it, and we need it now. This will enable us to serve our customers better, make more sales and forecast more accurately for the coming financial year. Imagine if things were easier and less scary because we knew more about our customers. So: How could we make things better with the CRM? What might that look like?"

"Is this what the stuff last week was about?" asked Amy. "Why was it so complicated?"

The team dug into the details together. Mark led a brainstorm about what kind of info they wanted to collect from customers, and when that information would be the most useful. Carlos suggested finding birthdays and hobbies and adding those into the CRM. Tyler suggested that there'd be a lot online from networking websites that could potentially be used. Getting it at the right time would mean setting up some alerts before birthdays, and bringing up personal profiles whenever someone called or when they were preparing for a meeting. They had some tactics that they could use. Mark left the meeting feeling recharged.

Later that day, on the drive home, Mark wondered why the team had finally bought into using the CRM when previously they had been so resistant. What had been different this time? He had the same people in the room – people with the same tools and abilities they had had a week ago. As far as Mark could tell, the only difference was how he had talked about the work.

Last time, he came at the team with a lot; he had presented everything that needed to be done. This time he had distilled his plan into six words. The team seemed to be able to grasp the idea much more easily and had even looked excited at the idea of and painting a picture of a better future.

Mark pulled into his driveway and stopped the car. He reached into his bag, pulled out his notebook, and turned to a new page. He needed to document this, so he didn't forget to do it next time. But what had he actually done differently?

He sat thinking for a few moments while the engine cooled and ticked away. *The team didn't flinch when I suggested the CRM – well, the second time. I distilled the problem into a simple, easily understood idea. And I got them on board by getting them to imagine how we could do things better.*

Mark looked down at the notebook and drew a big circle. Inside it he wrote *Curiosity*.

EN PASSANT

Mark pulled into the driveway and found John at the door. A week had passed since their last game.

"John, how are you? Have you had Baxter out for a walk?"

"Yes, and what a well-behaved dog he is," John laughed. "He only threatened one small dog and its attached septuagenarian."

"He must be slowing down, huh."

"Another game of chess tonight?" John gestured towards his house on the hill. "Must be your turn to win!"

"Must be. That sounds great. Actually, I wouldn't mind bouncing an idea off you, if you're up for it? A lot has happened this week."

"Interesting. See you at eight?"

"Perfect." Mark gave John a wave and turned to walk into the house.

Patricia was sitting at the table, working. "How's the writing going, Patty?" Mark asked.

"I'm struggling to concentrate at the moment and it's affecting my writing." Patricia closed her laptop. "I want to discuss something with you, but I'm never sure when it's the right time. Now is as good as ever."

Mark waited, wondering what was on Patricia's mind.

"How's the business doing? I know you're working really hard, and that it's not easy. But I feel like I'm in the dark. I'm just waiting for you to tell me. It makes me very nervous. Is everything going to be OK?"

Mark didn't know what to say. He didn't want to lie to her, but he wasn't exactly sure what the truth was. He certainly didn't want Patricia to worry, but it seemed keeping her in the dark was not helping either.

"I don't know. I wish I could be more definite, and I definitely wish I could be more positive. We are OK this month, I think. I'm trying to put better business practices in place, but they will take longer to realize a benefit in the business. The team seems on board with things, but we're not seeing any results yet. Do you remember when I told you about the idea of building a flywheel?"

Patricia nodded. "The one that shoots snowballs at battleships that are in the wrong seat on the bus?"

Mark laughed. "Yes, that's the one. By adding momentum to the 'flywheel' we can achieve better and better results. Like a snowball gathering momentum as it rolls down the hill."

Patricia's eyes had already started to glaze over.

"Forget the snowball," Mark continued. "What I am trying to do is improve a number of small things across the business. Each one adds momentum to the flywheel and should produce better results down the road."

"Is it working?" asked Patricia.

Mark hesitated. "If you had asked me yesterday, I would have said no, but after today I can confidently say *perhaps*."

"Are we going to have to sell the house?"

Patricia's question hung in the air. Mark wasn't sure. Yet.

"It's OK if we do have to," Patricia added. "I've been thinking about it. We can downsize and move closer to Mom."

Mark laughed. "Is that the encouragement I need to stop the business from failing – the looming threat of being closer to your mom?"

Patricia laughed. "You love Mom!"

"At a distance, yes. Next door, maybe not so much. We'll work through this, I'm sure. I'll work on being more communicative about where we are at with the business. If I'm being honest, I think I have been avoiding thinking about it myself."

Mark gave Patricia a hug. "Thanks for your support. I really appreciate it. I hope you can get back to your writing. I'm gonna grab a sandwich and then head up for a game of chess with John. I'll be back by ten."

ROOK TAKES KING'S PAWN

John knocked over his king, resigning the game. He reached over to shake Mark's hand.

"Great game, you really had me on the run there at the end. Have you been practicing while I'm not watching?"

Mark laughed. "No, I haven't been practicing. Thanks for the game. It's good to win one at last. By the way, I tried your suggestion with the team."

John looked puzzled. "Which suggestion was that?" he asked.

"When we played chess last week, you asked me to work out why the team didn't like my ideas."

"Did I?" John smiled.

"Didn't you?" Now Mark was confused. "'Well, that's what I did. I realized that I was presenting them with everything all at once, and that I hadn't done the work of distilling the idea down to its core. I tried a different approach this morning and the team were much more receptive."

"That's great news, Mark. So, everything is fixed now?"

John's face gave nothing away. Mark paused. When John asked questions like that, he was sure he was trying to help him dig deeper.

"Hmm, well I thought it was, but now I'm not so sure."

"How will you know it's worked?"

John had Mark firmly in his sights now. There was no squirming away.

"Um, when I get the results I need? When the team is happy?

When the team gets the results they need? When we make a profit again? All of these? Something completely different?" Mark felt frazzled. "I'm not clear on what success looks like, am I? And if *I'm* not clear, how can the team succeed?" He shook his head and looked down at his watch. "I had better head home. I think I have a lot of work to do tomorrow."

John chuckled. "Let me know how it goes. I'm always here for a game of chess and bouncing ideas."

On the walk home, Mark began to think about what he needed to do next. He needed to know what the team had achieved and get their feedback.

A PROCESS OF DISCOVERY

Mark stopped by Ryan's desk first thing in the morning.

"Ry, would you say you have a pretty good idea of what's going on in the office? Whether people are happy, if someone is struggling or if someone is doing well?"

"Sure. I don't know exactly what is happening, but I think I have the vibe, if you know what I mean."

Mark thought he did. "Good, good. So how would you say the new CRM initiative is going?"

Ryan suddenly looked down at his wrist and tapped an imaginary watch. "Gosh, is that the time?"

Mark grimaced. "That can't be good." He wanted his team to be honest with him.

"It's not great," said Ryan. "The team is starting to use the CRM, but they don't know why or if they are doing what is needed. They are a bit frustrated. They don't want to disappoint you. No one wants Mark's 'disappointed face'."

"I don't have a 'disappointed face'! Do I?"

Ryan raised his eyebrows, his eyes growing wide. "Sure, you don't," he said.

"Is this my 'disappointed face'?" Mark tried to keep any emotion from reaching his face.

"That's the one. Turn it off, turn it off!" Ryan shied away like a vampire caught in the morning sun. Mark laughed.

"OK, OK, I get it. It's bad. I'll add that to the to-do list. Back to the CRM: I'm wondering if one of the reasons the team is confused is that they don't know what success looks like. I would like to work through that today and share it with them this afternoon. What do you think?"

Ryan shrugged. "I have no idea. Perhaps you should just try and see what happens?"

A SWING AND A …

Mark spent the rest of the morning and most of the afternoon working through a description of success for the team. He read blog posts, listened to a podcast, considered the lead and lag indicators, and wondered whether he had 'the right people on the bus'.

Eventually Mark realized that getting information into the CRM wasn't actually the goal. It was just a step along the way. There were two key things that the team needed to do and therefore that they needed to measure.

The first was the level of activity – how often they were contacting clients and potential clients.

The second was the impact of this activity – the extent to which it was generating sales. They could have all the information in the world in the CRM, but it wouldn't help. They needed activity, and they needed sales.

It was simple, and it was clear. This could work! Mark was impatient to share it with the team. He asked Ryan to get the team together once again.

Everyone was in the conference room when Mark walked in. He gave everyone a big smile and was rewarded with three smiles and one set of crossed arms. Seventy-five percent – that's a solid B+.

"First I'd like to apologize," Mark began. This was becoming a habit. "I want to take you on the journey with me, but we've set sail before I've charted our course. I need to decide our direction of travel while we are still on land."

"Are we heading out onto the harbor?" asked Jane, looking a bit confused.

"Yes, that's right," Mark continued with his metaphor, pleased that Jane was getting on board. "We are heading out of the harbor, but this time we're going to set the course before we set sail."

Mark's analogies didn't always land well with the team, and he felt a stab of pride that this one had surely hit the mark.

He looked around the room. Jane seemed pleased, Carlos was drawing on his pad, Tyler appeared nervous, and Amy still had her arms crossed. He pressed on.

"I've been focusing on the wrong thing. It's really important that we understand why we are using the CRM and what success looks like. I have come up with two numbers that we can track that will help us stay on course and measure our success.

"First, we should measure our sales activity, and second, the results. If we are doing enough of the first, we will see an improvement in the second."

Mark paused. "Does that make sense?"

Around the room everyone was nodding in unison, like the Yoda bobble head on Mark's desk when he was typing.

"Great. Are there any questions?"

"When are we going to get more sales? Isn't doing this just a distraction?" Amy asked.

Mark realized that he hadn't quite unpacked this as much as he needed to. "The second measurement is the results – that is our sales. So, the point of this is to get more sales. In fact, the idea is that we can remove distractions to focus on this."

Amy looked skeptical.

"So, we are going to measure how much information we put into the CRM and then that will turn into sales?" It was Tyler's turn to look confused. "How does the CRM make sales?"

"No, the CRM doesn't make the sales. The goal isn't entering information into the CRM. The goal is more sales activity."

Mark was nodding and smiling at Tyler. 'Disappointed face' wasn't getting a look in today.

"Ok, I get it." Tyler didn't look like he'd got it.

"Is everyone as excited as I am?" Mark enthused.

"We couldn't be more excited!" said Carlos, looking a little less than excited. Mark decided to take it as a win.

THERE'S ALWAYS MONEY IN THE SPREADSHEET

Amy knocked on Mark's office door.

"Can we talk?"

Mark looked up from his laptop. "Of course. What's up, Amy?"

Amy stood in the doorway. "I'm worried. I ran the cashflow projections that you asked for, and I think that within six weeks we won't be able to make payroll. We just don't have enough money coming in – even with Rick's order back up to half what it was. Can you have a look?"

"Come over. Let's have a look at this together. There's always money in the spreadsheet!" Mark said cheerfully.

Mark and Amy pored over the spreadsheet for the next half hour. They brought forward some invoices and looked at what bills they could delay. They didn't find any 'new' money – but they were at least getting a more accurate view of what things looked like, and they found a couple of small errors in their favor. They could definitely make it through this month, and probably the month after. But the month following was looking bad. Amy was right. All their cash reserves would be gone, and they would have trouble meeting payroll.

"Well, that's bought us some time." Mark was trying to put on a positive spin. "Can you get those invoices out this week?"

Amy still looked worried, but at least now Mark understood the situation they were in. "I'll send through a message once the invoices are off and we have an idea of when they might be paid. Could we catch up again in a few days and see what else we can do?"

"Great idea," agreed Mark.

Everything was OK, for now. The future was less clear.

A RUDE AWAKENING

Mark looked at his phone. It was just after three in the morning. He had been lying awake for the last hour, going over numbers in his head. There was something bothering him, but he wasn't sure what.

Whatever it was, it wasn't going to let him sleep any time soon. Mark slipped out of bed, grabbed a T-shirt off the floor and padded down to the living room. He switched on the small lamp beside the couch, opened his laptop and fired up the spreadsheet. There was only one spreadsheet, and by this point it ran the whole business. It had evolved over the course of ten years and had become an indispensable tool to help Mark see everything that was going on.

Mark didn't know what he was looking for, but he knew that something wasn't right. He started going through the spreadsheet, checking, and double-checking every number and every calculation.

It took him 20 restless minutes to find what had been bothering him. A misplaced zero in one of the calculations meant that next month's revenue was overstated by more than $50,000. Mark sank back into the couch, put the laptop to one side and stared at the TV that was sitting like a black window to nowhere on the wall in front of him. He felt lost.

"Hey," Patricia said softly from the door of the living room. "You OK?"

Mark didn't know how long he had been sitting and staring at the wall.

"Yep, all good. Well not good – bad. I couldn't sleep. Something was bothering me, so I got up and started going through the spreadsheet. I found a problem, and I'm not sure how to solve it."

"Is there anything I can do?" asked Patricia tentatively.

"I don't think so, Patty."

Patricia sat down beside Mark and put her arm around his shoulders. "Shall we go back to bed?"

"Yes, I guess we should."

Mark drifted in and out of sleep until the bleating alarm woke him and Patty.

Showered and dressed, Mark didn't feel much better than he did at three that morning. Over a coffee at the kitchen bench, Patty said, "I've found a house for sale. It's a bit smaller and it's not by the beach. But it's in a good neighborhood and it's not any closer to Mom."

Mark laughed at the joke, but knew that Patricia's thinking had some merit. "Tell me more about how far it is from your Mom."

"I've had a look at the market, and I think that if we downsize, we can free up some money to put into the business. I know that it's not the dream, but we will get through this." Patricia was clearly trying to be upbeat. "We could take a look at it tomorrow?"

"Patty, what would I do without you? Book it in. I had better head to work, break the bad news to Amy, and get working on some sales."

"Amy's going to be worried, so make sure you look after her."

Mark nodded and smiled. He suspected Amy focused on money because it was something she was good at – and doing what she was good at was her way of showing she cared.

He grabbed his laptop from the couch, where he had left it the night before.

"I know, I know. I'll look after her."

REFLECTION

Mark was feeling the pressure. He'd worked hard to provide for his family, and now they were looking to sell the house. He'd created a plan to get sales going again, but he had a suspicion that the team were still struggling to understand what was needed.

Time for some reflection. Tearing off a page from the pad on his desk, Mark started to draw circles and lines, making a mind map of the journey so far.

His first attempt to kick-start sales had been to learn as much as he could and to get the team to join him on the journey. Mark wrote *LEARN* and circled it. But while the book had been useful for Mark, it hadn't meant much to the team. They hadn't been in the same place. In fact, they were possibly all in different places. He hadn't stopped to ensure the team recognized the relevance of reading the book, that they had the time needed to do the learning or that he understood where they were in terms of understanding the concepts in it.

His second attempt was to design a system based around the CRM, and then get the team to implement it. This had been a bit of a disaster. If he were honest, a complete disaster. It didn't take a lot of reflection to work out what had gone wrong here. It was too big and too complicated. Because the team hadn't been involved in designing the solution, it also bore no relation to the way they worked or what they needed. Mark created a column on the left of the page titled *DIDN'T WORK*. Below this he wrote *Imposing systems from above*.

His third approach had been to simplify the initiative – to be clear about the problem and the successful solution. Mark felt that this had been a turning point, and that the team had finally understood why they needed to get on the bus and where they were going.

Mark looked at the page in front of him. He was starting to see some patterns. Having a team that was engaged and involved with a solution – a team that was curious about how best to go about making changes – seemed to be the best place to start. *But there was also a need to make sure they could make changes without tanking their momentum.*

He wrote *THE PROBLEM* underneath *LEARN*, and then wrote *DESTINATION* beneath that. He circled them both.

It was time to see how the team was doing.

CHECK IN

Mark spent the rest of the morning gathering information. He looked at the team's activity in the CRM and at sales over the last few weeks. He could see that the team was making more use of the system, but not at the level he had expected. At this rate he couldn't see sales coming through in time to save the business. He needed to find out how each team member was feeling and why they weren't able to lift the sales effort, so he asked Ry to set up meetings with each of the leadership team.

His first catch up was with Jane. After some small talk, Mark got down to business.

"Jane, how are you finding our new sales push? Are you managing to find ways to support Tyler and Carlos?"

Jane was clearly surprised. "Isn't that Tyler's role? I mean he is the salesperson. I don't do sales, so I thought I was just…"

"Watching?" That frustration bubbled up again.

"Yes, I do *support* them. But more in spirit than in body." Jane laughed nervously. "I'm not sure how I could help with sales anyway. Not really my thing."

Mark thanked Jane. This hadn't been the most satisfactory conversation. He wondered if he was on the path to getting an ulcer. Maybe his next conversation with Tyler would make him feel more confident about the future.

For a change of scene, Tyler and Mark sat on the couches near the break room. The sun was streaming in through windows that faced out to the park. Mark could see pigeons huddling around a family having a picnic. Tyler put down his coffee.

"Sales are going great!" he exclaimed. "Well not actual sales, but you know, *sales*."

Mark didn't know. "Do you mean we have been making new sales?"

"Oh no – no new sales, but I meant, you know, that the sales role is going great." Tyler's smile looked a little forced.

Mark still didn't understand what Tyler was trying to say, so he tried to dig a little deeper. "Do you mean that we have increased our sales activity, reached out to more customers, and built better relationships?"

Tyler nodded vigorously. "Yep, all of that. All. Of. That."

"Great, that's really great. So, we're seeing more sales coming through? Because the sales pipeline hasn't changed in the last few weeks."

"Yes, loads more sales. Soon, there will be loads more. There is bound to be, right?" Tyler was still nodding.

"So, there are no new sales you know of, currently," Mark asked, suspecting he knew the answer.

Tyler kept nodding.

"No, no yet." Tyler's nodding was starting to slow. "But, you know, soon."

Mark signed inwardly. "Thanks Tyler, that's great. Keep up the good work." He was starting to get a picture of where they were at, and it wasn't pretty.

Mark walked over to Carlos's office and knocked on his open door.

"Hey boss, what's up?"

"Just catching up with everyone to check on how we're going with the sales initiative," Mark said as he sat down next to Carlos's desk.

"And how is everyone going?" Carlos asked.

"I was hoping you could tell me," Mark answered. "How do you think we're doing?"

"Well, that's a good question. What are we meant to be

doing, again? I'm not sure I'm 100 percent clear on this sales initiative. Um, I mean, I know we need more sales, and I know we're measuring activity in the CRM, but what is it that you want *me* to do?"

MONEYPENNY

Mark and Amy sat at the meeting table together, Mark's laptop open in front of them, and the spreadsheet pulled up on the screen. Mark skipped through the spreadsheet, checking formulas, and moving numbers. Occasionally he turned to Amy to clarify a number or a date.

"Well, I think that's it." Mark sat back in his chair. "I can't find any extra money or any more savings. How about you?"

Amy scanned the spreadsheet again. "No, I think we have found everything. It's looking... tight," she said, clearly choosing her words carefully.

Mark sighed. There wasn't any more money in the spreadsheet. And soon there wouldn't be any more money in the bank. Then he thought about what Patricia had said last week.

"How are you feeling, Amy?"

"I'm worried. This is stressful. I don't like it." Amy looked at Mark as if he might say something insightful and encouraging. But Mark couldn't. His optimism was taking a severe battering, and he struggled to find the words to make Amy feel better.

"It's a bit rubbish, isn't it? I'm sure we will find a way, though."

Amy nodded. Mark couldn't tell if it was from agreement, or because there wasn't any other response to make. He closed the lid of his laptop and put it in his bag. "I'll have a chat with Patricia and see what we can do."

It was quiet when Mark walked into the house later that day.

Mark put down his bag and wandered into the kitchen. Patty and Luke were out – probably down at the beach enjoying the early evening sun. Luke always came back home with a new stick or two to add to his collection. Mark wasn't sure what made a stick worthy of addition to the collection, but Luke certainly knew. Baxter was less picky, so Luke's stick collection had to be stored well out of the dog's reach.

Thinking of Baxter, Mark realized that he hadn't had a greeting from him either. Baxter must be out with John. Perhaps John would be around for chess this evening. Mark really needed some advice.

He stood at the window looking out over the nearby houses to the sea. The sun was starting to set, bathing the whole scene in a fire-red light. Patty and Luke burst through the door downstairs and into the house. Luke was explaining loudly to Patty about the fine qualities of the stick he had found.

Mark smiled. Hearing Patty and Luke downstairs filled him with joy and appreciation. He was very grateful for his family and the life he had. Mark sighed. They were going to miss the beach.

MOVIE TIME

A week had passed since Mark had spoken to the team and gathered their thoughts on processes. He'd rebounded in the last few days, and was cautiously excited about this morning's meeting.

He had a plan. He had spent the previous afternoon thinking about his team and what they needed to get on board with this new idea: Meetings – and better ones at that. Mark had found a short video online with a well-respected business coach talking through the idea of building better meetings by improving how teams approached their agendas. It was simple, but Mark could see that there were some subtleties that could make this transformational for the business.

The video itself wasn't going to be enough, though. Mark had to get the team engaged in the idea and what it would mean for the business. He would need to help them on the journey.

He considered who was going to be around the table this morning, and how they liked information presented to them. Carlos liked to talk ideas through. Tyler wanted the big picture. Amy needed all the details to feel comfortable. For Jane, it had to be engaging.

By the time of the meeting, Ryan had moved the presentation screen into the room, and the team sat around the table looking at Mark expectantly. He took a deep breath and smiled.

"I thought I would try something new today. I've come across an idea that, I think, can help us and I want to take you through it. I've got a video that explains the idea. We will watch this together and then we can have a chat about what we learned. How does that sound?"

The team nodded, except Jane, who looked concerned.

"Does that sound OK to you, Jane?" Mark asked.

"I'm wondering, how long is the video? Is it like, an hour?" Jane started to look towards the exit.

"It's under five minutes," Mark said with renewed enthusiasm.

"Oh, fantastic!" exclaimed Jane as she sat back in her chair.

Mark sat down at the table with the others and reached for the mouse and keyboard. After a little fiddling, the video started.

The coach was on stage and started explaining the big picture of the idea and how it had helped two of the organizations she had coached. Mark let it run for a minute as the coach explained the main principle of team-defined agendas. He paused the video.

"So that's the big picture. I thought it might be a good place to stop and see if you had any questions and I wondered whether you thought this might work for us?"

Amy was the first to speak. "I think it would help us a lot. It would make our weekly meeting more interesting and efficient. I am very interested to know exactly what we need to do."

"Thanks, Amy. Anyone else?"

There were questions from Carlos and Tyler, and some enthusiastic nodding from Jane. The questions generated a short but interesting conversation about the value fixed agendas for team meetings might add. Mark pressed play again on the video and the coach on screen continued her explanation.

The coach dived into the details of the process, explaining each part of the recommended meeting agenda and how each team could shape theirs. Mark paused the video again and invited more discussion. He encouraged the team to answer each other's questions and to take the time needed to make sure everyone fully understood the concept. He asked the team to think of examples from around the organization where the idea might work – situations where they were already using these ideas and what that meant for those teams and situations.

The video ended with some on-screen applause, and Mark turned off the screen. The team were already starting to excitedly share ideas and suggestions for implementing the new process. Mark walked over to the whiteboard and picked up a marker, but instead of starting to write, he turned and walked back to the table.

"Carlos, can you lead us through a brainstorm to capture what we learned and what actions we are going to take?" He handed the marker to Carlos.

"Uh, yep. That would be great!" Carlos exclaimed as he got out of his chair and walked up to the board. Mark took a seat with the rest of the team.

Carlos led the team through a great brainstorming session, Mark thought. They created a short list of actions they each wanted to take to implement the new meeting format.

"That's it." Carlos smiled, putting the marker pen back in its tray. He stepped back from the board. The plan looked good.

Mark looked around the room, everyone looked engaged and energized. Success!

"Thanks everyone, I am looking forward to giving this a go! Jane, you have the first action on the board: Writing up the new agenda. Is there anything standing in your way?"

Jane shook her head, "No, I'm good to go. I will have it written up and sent to everyone by the end of the day."

"Thanks Jane." Mark said, smiling back at her. The team packed up their belongings and filed out of the room to get on with their day. Mark thanked each of them as they walked out the door.

For the first time in a long time, Mark felt hopeful as the meeting ended.

As he packed his satchel for the trip home, he reflected on what had worked when introducing this latest idea to the team. As far as he could see, the biggest change was that he had taken a lot more care to explain the idea; he had made sure that everyone understood. But what else? Using a video with an expert certainly helped. And Mark had taken the time to use examples, so that the team could clarify the idea in their mind. It was the first time he could look around the table and really see that each of his team had understood what he was proposing.

I think I made the idea understandable, and each of the team could connect it to previous ideas and experiences they'd had. So it was more than understandable, they were also able to use the information and the idea.

He pulled out his notebook, and turned to the page where he had drawn the big circle with *Curiosity* written within it. He drew a new circle that intersected with the first, and inside it he wrote the word *Accessible*.

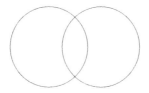

AND WE'RE BACK IN THE ROOM

Mark was pleased with how the team had taken to the new meeting format. He wasn't able to make every meeting over the month, as he was still pounding the pavement meeting potential clients. But in the meetings that he got to, the team was following the new agenda. Well, mostly. They still needed some prompting, but he felt like they were on board.

Today was the weekly leadership team meeting. Mark made an effort to get to the room early so that he could write up the new agenda on the whiteboard. He hadn't been at the leadership team meeting for a couple of weeks, and was eager to hear how it had been going for the team.

Carlos was the first to arrive. Mark greeted him with a smile. Carlos glanced over at the board and then sat down. Amy and Tyler came in together chatting about their day and Jane arrived soon after.

Mark was getting ready to start when Amy spoke up.

"We need to talk about sick days. They are really impacting our ability to get orders out the door," she launched.

"Ahh, thank you Amy, that does sound like a problem." Mark replied. He glanced around the room, everyone was staring at him. "First, why don't we follow the agenda and we can talk about this in the fourth section, if it is the most important thing that comes up?"

Amy did not look happy. "It is the most important! We don't get paid unless our customers get their orders!"

"I agree, Amy; that does sound important. Can it wait until

we get to that part of the meeting?"

"No. This has to come first." Amy sat with crossed arms. Her roots were planted.

Jane started talking about who was taking leave and why. Carlos stared out the window. Tyler was on his phone under the table.

Mark could see that the meeting was not going to go as planned. He took a deep breath and dived into the conversation about sick days and orders.

The meeting came to an end as everyone started to check their phones and murmur about other commitments. The team began to leave the room.

Mark caught Carlos's attention as he stood to leave, "Carlos, can I catch up with you for a few minutes?"

Carlos looked around the room and glanced behind Mark. *Was Carlos looking for a way out?*

"Of course, always time for a chat," smiled Carlos, weakly. He sat back down at the table.

"I just wanted to see how the new meeting agenda has been going. The team didn't really seem committed to it today. Does everyone understand it?"

Carlos nodded furiously. "Yes, we all understand it and it has been useful, really useful, super useful." Carlos paused, visibly searching for what to say next. Mark jumped in.

"So today was an exception? You have been using it in your meetings when I haven't been there?"

Carlos was looking back over his shoulder towards the door as Mark finished. "Yes, 100 percent, I mean, why wouldn't we? It makes perfect sense. I would say we have made small tweaks here and there but definitely, like, 95 percent of it, every time. Most of the time, 95 percent, sometimes less, but we are really working on it. So, yeah, great."

Mark felt pleased, but also a bit confused. He trusted Carlos though, so Mark thanked him as they both stood and left the room.

Later, Mark met with Amy after lunch to work on the spreadsheet. They managed to find a few thousand dollars in the month's billing that could go out early. *There is always money in the spreadsheet*, Mark thought, chuckling to himself. As they finished up, Mark decided to verify his conversation with Carlos.

"Just before you head off, Amy, I want to check something with you."

Amy closed the lid on her laptop and sat back in her chair.

"Is this about today's meeting? Because that stuff is super important, and we really need to pay more attention to it. I seem to be the only one that cares! I know you care about it, but I really need more support on this."

Mark could see that Amy was frustrated. Her heart was in the right place.

"It *is* about today's meeting, but it's not about that. I had a quick conversation with Carlos after the meeting and he reassured me that, when I'm not there, the meetings are running with the new agenda. Which is great!" Mark looked closely to gauge Amy's reaction.

"Of course he did." Amy crossed her arms. "You know that he doesn't want to see 'disappointed face'. Carlos is notoriously bad at delivering bad news. You know the rest of the team call him *El Flanderino*."

Mark looked confused.

Amy continued. "Ned Flanders. He's always so optimistic. He can't ever tell you bad news."

"But Carlos doesn't have a mustache?"

Amy carried on. "We tried to follow the agenda, but actually we have some things that are just too important. What if the agenda doesn't work? Then important things are going to fall through the cracks!"

Mark worked hard to remain composed. "Thanks Amy. It looks like I have a bit of thinking to do."

Amy's arms remained crossed.

CHECKMATE

Mark sat facing John across the chess board – a study in concentration as their minds looked for patterns and options. John's focus was on the pieces in front of him, but Mark was focused on his cashflow crisis. He still wasn't seeing the change he wanted. *Where was the gap now?* The team were interested in making changes; he'd seen them make changes safely with the processes – but they hadn't got results. He'd seen how they'd really connected with the ideas in the meeting agenda video and had tried to implement them – but they weren't really clear or committed to them. Where was the team struggling? And why?

Mark needed more information so that he could discover what the team really needed to succeed.

"I think that's mate," said John as he moved his rook to the back rank of the board. Mark came back to the room and the game in front of him.

"It looks that way, well done." There wasn't much congratulation in Mark's voice.

"Everything OK, Mark? You seem off-form today."

Mark wanted to ask for help, but the stakes seemed so high that he was struggling to put his needs into words.

"I'm thinking a lot about work and family at the moment."

"Would you like to share? I won't have the answers, but it might be good to talk about it."

Mark cleared his throat. "There are three things, and they are related. First, we are running out of cash in the business.

Second, we are looking at selling the house to keep the business afloat. And third, I can't seem to get the team on board with making changes to how we work." Mark took a deep breath. "It feels like a lot."

"It sounds like a lot." John was nodding. "What do you think is going to happen?"

"I think selling the house will be OK. It will be sad and a bit stressful, but I'm lucky that Patty understands – it was even her suggestion. This will definitely keep the lights on at work, but if I can't start making some changes to the way we work, we are going to be right back where we are now, sooner rather than later." Mark stopped. He did feel a bit better, though he was daunted by the amount that was going on.

John took a moment to respond.

"So, you have a short-term problem – the cashflow crisis – for which you've found a solution: Selling the house. But you are worried that you have a systemic problem that will impact your business's ability to survive in the long term?"

"You make it sound simple! That does sum it up nicely. You work with a lot of business leaders. What would you tell them?"

John sat back in his chair. "Mark, you know I don't have any answers. But if you are up for it, I could ask you some questions that I think might help."

"Please!"

John chuckled. "I have three questions for you, but don't try to answer them now.

"The first question is: Are you looking to completely overhaul how your business works or are you taking a small step on a journey of change?

"The second question is: How does your team and the wider organization feel about change?

"And, finally: In your organization, is it OK to try and not succeed?"

Mark laughed. "I see we are starting with the easy questions!"

He tried to smile but looked instead like he might have stood on some Lego. "I feel like there might be right and wrong answers to these questions."

"It might feel like that," answered John. "But to get value from them, you will need to find your answers. If you can answer these questions honestly, you might get some clarity on what to do next. You know what they say: *Qiānlǐ zhī xíng, shǐyú zú xià.*"

"Always good to be playing chess with Confucius. My Mandarin is a bit rusty; what is that in English?"

"A journey of a thousand miles begins with a single step."

REFLECTION

Mark pulled out his notebook and looked at John's questions as he'd written them down the previous night. *Was he looking to make a full-scale sweeping change to the business, or was he looking for a small, incremental step change?* While there were a lot of challenges that needed solving, Mark felt that the way the business was structured was fundamentally sound. It was more a case of trying to level everything up – not changing it completely. Well, at least not overnight.

Mark thought about what had worked in the past. He'd had more success with small, incremental changes. Any time he had tried to make a big change he'd fallen flat on his face. He was pretty sure he had the answer to question number one: He was looking for a small incremental change. That reminded Mark of the flywheel in the book he had read. Or was it the snowball? He would have to have another look. Mark wrote: *Small incremental change*.

Mark looked at the second question: *How does everyone feel about change?* He was puzzled by this one. Shouldn't the team welcome change if it was good for the business? Mark loved change, and he got bored very easily. But John was encouraging him to find the answers rather than work out what the questions meant, so perhaps he should trust the process. Mark was always encouraging the team to trust the process. It was time to take some of his own advice. He needed to talk to the team. Mark wrote: *Talk to Ryan and Carlos*.

The third question was easier. Mark thought he knew the

answer. *In your organization, is it OK to try and not succeed?* Of course, people could try and fail. As long as it wasn't a big failure, and it wasn't with a customer or a potential customer, and it didn't affect profit or revenue, and it didn't inconvenience Mark. Right. Maybe it wasn't so safe. He needed to check with the team on this one too it seemed. Mark wrote: *Ditto*.

This morning was going to be interesting.

CHANGING TACK

Mark caught Ryan in the kitchen. "Morning Ry, how's it going?"

"It's going great boss. You want a coffee?" Ryan was pouring a mug for himself and grabbed another, offering it to Mark.

"Sure, thanks. Hey, I have a couple of questions I would love to run past you. I think they might be really important," said Mark.

"Sure, should we grab a seat? Is everything OK?"

"Yes, yes, everything is great." Mark sat at the table and Ryan joined him. "How do you feel about change in the business?"

Ryan laughed. "Do you know the first thing Amy said to me when I joined? 'I hope you like change!' I wasn't quite sure what she meant. But since the day I started nothing has happened but change."

Ryan was smiling. Mark thought that was probably a good sign.

"It sounds like I should have a chat with Amy as well." Mark was surprised by Ryan's answer, though he hadn't really answered the question. "But how do you *feel* about the change?"

"Well…" Ryan was weighing his words carefully. "Sometimes I feel fatigued by the amount of change, and other times we don't follow through very well. Often, we haven't finished one change before we come up with another. That can make me feel a bit like, *What's the point?* It can be…" Ryan paused.

"Exciting?" Mark interjected.

"Exhausting." Ryan finished his thought.

"Oh." Mark felt despondent. He loved change and coming up with ideas. He was disappointed that the team – or at least Ryan – wasn't as enthusiastic about it as he was.

"Was there another question?" asked Ryan.

"Maybe later. I think I should have a chat to Amy and maybe Carlos. You know, to get a range of views. Thanks, Ry. I appreciate your honesty."

Mark found Carlos in his office working at his laptop. Mark knocked on the open door and waited for Carlos to look up.

"Hey Mark, come in. How's your day going?"

"Not bad," said Mark, wishing he could say it was going great. "Just catching up with a few of the team here and there to clarify things."

"Great, how can I help?" Carlos asked. He began to nod furiously for some reason. Mark ignored the nodding and launched straight into his question.

"Do you think we have a culture where it is OK to try new things, even if they don't work?"

Carlos blurted out a laugh – then stopped once he saw that Mark's face had dropped. "Yes, well, sort of. I mean if people don't mind seeing your 'disappointed face'. Ha ha! I mean no."

Mark was disappointed, and his face showed it. He needed clarity from Carlos.

"In conclusion, generally speaking, it's *not* OK to try and fail?"

"We want to try things, but everything always seems so important – too important – to fail. I think we end up not wanting to do new things," admitted Carlos.

Mark sighed. "Got it, I understand. Thanks for giving it to me straight, Carlos." Mark knew his 'disappointed face' was being replaced by a 'sad face'.

"Well, I had better get back to... it." Carlos gestured at the screen in front of him, where he had his browser open on his favorite music news website.

Mark made it back to his desk. He ran through the last two conversations in his head. Ryan had told him about how change felt constant and fatiguing. Carlos had shared that it wasn't safe to try and fail. In both conversations, the issue came back to Mark and how he led the team. Still, that was only the perspective of two of the team. Who else could give him honest, direct, feedback?

He made a beeline for Amy's office, and took a moment to appear as relaxed as possible when he appeared at her door.

"Amy, do you have a second?"

"Sure, Mark. Come on in." Amy was scrutinizing the spreadsheet.

"What would it be like if, as an organization, we were able to make a series of small incremental changes to the way we worked, in an environment where the team felt safe to experiment with new things, and we just did one thing at a time?"

Amy's eyes widened. Mark felt that he'd blurted too much out at once.

"It would be amazing! We would be so successful!" Amy said. She leaned forward. "It would be unicorns flying over rainbows pooping gold!"

Mark burst out laughing. "That's quite the image Amy. You really think it would be that good?"

Amy laughed. "I really do!"

Mark wrapped up with Amy, then walked back to his office and sat down behind his desk. Reaching down to his bag, he pulled out his notebook. He turned to the page where he had drawn the big circles.

He could see that the *size* of the change was important. But it wasn't the size itself that mattered. *That's what this was about*, he realized. The size of the change was important because it made it safer to fail, but it was that safety that was critical. It was how he made the team *feel*. He had to create a container they could try and fail in, without feeling like it was the end of the world.

He was excited. He had, what he thought was, the last piece of the puzzle. His notebook sat open in front of him on his desk. Two roughly drawn circles intersecting on the page. *Accessibility* written in one, and *Curiosity* in the other. Mark drew a third circle that intersected both circles. He laughed quietly to himself. *Wait till I show this to Patty,* he thought; *she loves a good Venn diagram.*

Mark drew a new circle that intersected the first two, and in it, he wrote *Safety.*

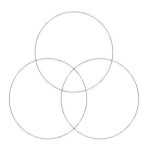

WHERE THE RUBBER MEETS THE ROAD

It had been quite the day, and as Mark trundled through the city streets and onto the highway, he mulled over the conversations from earlier. He had answers to John's questions. And it was becoming clear that if he wanted things to change, there was one person who had to improve their performance.

Mark pulled into the driveway of what was, for now, his home by the beach. There was a late model BMW parked in front of the house. That could mean only one thing: Carrie, their real estate agent, who'd sold them the house a few years ago.

He dropped his bag by the door and headed up the stairs. Patty and Carrie sat at the table looking over a laptop and a tablet. Carrie got to her feet to shake Mark's hand.

"Hiya Mark, how's things? Patty has just been showing me around. You've decorated it so well in the last few years! Miles different from when you first bought it."

Mark smiled, but his heart sank. They *were* giving up their dream house.

"Thanks, Carrie. We're looking forward to working with you again."

"Brilliant. Magnificent. And how's the business?"

Mark and Patricia exchanged a quick look. They didn't want to seem like 'motivated sellers.'

"Oh, you know," started Mark. "Keeping me busy!"

Patricia passed him the tablet. "This is a mockup for the house advertisement," she said, thankfully shifting the focus of the conversation.

He looked at the screen in front of him. The photo showed a beautiful house set by the beach. Their beautiful house.

"Looks great. We should buy it!" Mark joked, sighing inwardly.

"In the current market it will only take a couple of weeks to sell," Carrie explained. "I'm expecting that we will get at least two good offers. It's such a beautiful house, and perfect for a family."

Patricia turned to Mark. "Carrie thinks the place I found over on Hillside is a good option for us. That's the one that's a bit smaller but newer. It gets plenty of sun and is close to the new school. Carrie has offered to take us through later this evening."

Mark smiled. Patty was doing her best to make this as easy for them all as possible. "Let's do it," he said.

LEARNING

Mark had woken at five from a disturbing dream. His teeth were snapping off as he tried to eat a pancake. He was immediately thrown into thinking about the business. The future looked bleak. His world, in every sense of the word, was dark. He resolved to make a change. He was going to find a way out of this.

Mark sent a message to Ryan at sunrise. *Taking the day to do some learning. I'll see everyone tomorrow.*

Mark knew he didn't need to find the answers to all the problems he was facing. He just needed to work out how to embed small incremental changes into the business. One change, successfully executed, was the key. The longest journey starts with a single step.

He was going to spend the day re-reading the book with the bright yellow cover to find one thing. One thing that the team could try as an experiment and that, if it worked, would make a small but measurable impact on the business.

He needed the team's support and help to make changes. He had heard from Carlos, Ryan, and Amy that the team was tired from so many changes and ideas that went nowhere, and that they didn't feel safe trying new things.

Mark needed to find a change that the team felt comfortable with – one that they knew wouldn't break the company if it failed. Something they could learn from and use to take that learning to the next change.

He thought he understood now. As a company, they needed

to *learn* more, not *do* more. And in order to do the learning, Mark needed to make it safe for the team to experiment.

Mark worked through the book for the next few hours. He jotted down in his notebook every idea he came across that looked useful. By lunch he had a list of 15 ideas and a clear theme. The majority were about growing the team's skills and abilities, not increasing their capacity.

One idea stood out. Mark circled it and put down his pen.

After a moment, Mark opened flicked to the page with the Venn diagram. *Curiosity*, *Accessibility*, *Safety*. It made sense. But it wasn't enough that he *knew* what needed to be done; he needed to also ensure that what he did actually met each criteria of his model.

Mark turned to a new page. Methodically he worked out how he could get the team curious about the possibilities of this new idea and make sure it connected; it needed to be relevant, easy to understand, and easy to apply. Lastly, he thought about how he could make sure the team knew that, while he thought that this new idea might be a step change for them as a team, if it didn't work then that was fine; they would regroup and try something else. It wouldn't be the end of the world.

RE-SETTING THE SCENE

The team sat around the board table. Mark was struck by the familiarity of the scene. It was *The Last Supper* in business casual. The team looked relaxed, absent, agitated, and confused. Amy sat with her arms folded, her face determined. Carlos was browsing the web on his phone. Jane looked like she was thinking of cheese and crackers. Tyler was talking to Mark. Oh shoot, Tyler was talking to him.

"No news is good news," Tyler said. Mark had only caught the end of their conversation so chose to nod as though he understood.

"I'm sure the order will come through. We just have to give them some time." Tyler paused, clearly waiting for Mark to say something.

"I'm sure it will, I'm sure it will," Mark reassured Tyler.

Mark kicked off the meeting. "You might have noticed that I took yesterday to do some thinking and research. This was the result of a couple of conversations I had earlier in the week. I now realize that there is one person holding this company back and that they need to change or move on!"

Mark looked around the room. The team was suddenly very still. Amy still sat with her arms folded, her face remained set in a determined frown. Carlos stopped browsing the web and put down his phone. Jane's eyes were now as big as headlights. Tyler was looking nervously around the table.

"That person is me."

There were a number of audible sighs of relief.

"I have really let you and the company down. I have introduced too much change and change that hasn't been well thought-out. I have insisted on change without the support and follow-through to make it stick. I haven't created a space where we can try things and be comfortable that some of those things will fail." Mark took a deep breath. "I am sorry."

Some part of Mark secretly hoped someone would tell him he was wrong and that he had been doing a great job. This was a humbling experience for him.

"So, what's going to change?" Amy said. She could be relied on to ask the tough questions.

"I would like to change the way we approach change in the business. There are three things that I think are going to help.

"First, we are going to make one small, incremental change at a time.

"Second, we will treat each change as an experiment, not as a foregone conclusion.

"Third, we will ensure that if a change doesn't work, then we will have learnt something about the business, the market or ourselves. I want change to feel like learning, not failing.

"Imagine what things would be like if we got everything right – all our processes were getting great results, everyone knew what they needed to do next, and our pipeline of work was always growing. We'd each be working in our sweet spots, doing things we love; we'd be doing great work with our customers and helping them grow too. And we wouldn't be relying too much on one customer to fill our workload.

"It might seem far off, but we can get there if we make just one small change at a time. That's all it will take. One thing. If we all want to make things better, and we're making small, incremental changes, and we knew we were learning with each step, we'd feel pretty good about things. That's what I see."

Mark sat back in his chair. "What do you think?"

"I think that sounds good," Carlos started tentatively. "But sometimes we don't really understand your ideas or how they are going to help. We are left a bit confused. So how is this going to help?"

Mark was surprised. Carlos wasn't usually this direct. It looked like things were already moving in the right direction.

"Thanks, Carlos. That's a really useful observation. What do you think would help?"

"It would help us absorb the information if you could take a bit more time to unpack an idea and provide examples that we might already see in the business."

Mark looked around the room to see the others nodding.

"If I was able to make the ideas more accessible, as well as provide better examples, would it make it easier?"

The nodding continued.

"I have an idea for the first change we can try. It's just a small thing but I think it could make a difference if it works. It's from the book. Let me explain the idea, and then we can figure out if it's for us." Mark was feeling encouraged as he laid out his plan.

"The core idea is pretty simple. If we have better alignment as a leadership team, we will experience a number of benefits to the business. How do you think being better aligned could help us?" Mark asked the team.

Carlos was the first to answer. "Well, when the rest of the team asks us questions, they would get the same answer no matter which one of us they asked. That would make them feel safer and more confident in the leadership team."

Amy was next. "We would spend less time in meetings going over decisions that we thought we had already made."

There was a murmur of agreement from around the table.

"But how do we get alignment?" asked Tyler.

This was Mark's opportunity. The last time he tried to introduce a meeting agenda, there was a serious failure to launch. But what he realized was that he'd tried to push it on the team. If he could inspire the team with the agenda concept and make it – and its impact – clearer, then maybe it'd connect better.

"The book has many suggestions, but let's start with a simple one. We could adopt the book's sample agenda for our weekly management meeting and try it for a month or two to see if it helps our alignment. Using the agenda means we would cover the same things each week, with room for collecting and sharing feedback from the wider team and our clients. Actually, the operations team follow the same structured agenda every time they meet, and it's certainly helped them to get better alignment because the information is flowing better. This is a little bit like the suggestion from the video we watched – but this time, we're going to treat it as an experiment. If it doesn't improve our meetings after a couple of months, then we can try something else. What do you think?" Mark paused to make some space for the team.

Carlos looked encouraged. "So, we just try a new meeting agenda, and that's all?"

"Yes. The weekly meeting would be at the same time, on the same day. We will need to organize our other meetings around it. I'm hoping that thanks to this consistency, we will need fewer meetings overall" Mark replied.

Mark looked from person to person, trying to gauge how they were feeling and whether he had gone too far. Tyler looked relaxed but engaged. Carlos was smiling. Amy still sat with her arms folded, but without a frown on her face.

Jane summarized. "So we will be having a meeting every week, and it will be the same meeting?"

Mark nodded. "That's right. Does that make sense to you?"

Jane gave Mark a thumbs up. "Will we still be going on the fishing trip?"

Mark wasn't sure what Jane meant, but now wasn't the time to dampen the mood.

"Sure Jane! If after two months we've met every week and followed the same agenda, then how about we go on a fishing trip?"

The discussion continued for the next half hour. Mark introduced the team to the sample agenda, and they worked together to understand the purpose and potential benefit of each part of the agenda. By the end of the meeting, it felt like maybe now, finally, they were all on the same page – that they were working together. Things were going to be okay.

SIX MONTHS IN A LEAKY BOAT

It had been six months since their first successful change. It had been a simple change, but one that they could – and did – easily make. They set the team's leadership meeting for the same day and time each week, and with a constant agenda. That one small change had brought the leadership team together. Mark often remarked to Patty that it had been the spark that ignited the leadership team's curiosity.

It hadn't taken long for the team to fall into the new meeting pattern, and Mark noticed immediate results: The team was more engaged, and they managed to work through everything every week. He seemed to have more time at hand. He had heard the wider team remarking on how the leadership team "were all on the same page now." That one, small change had been a huge win.

He had noticed a change in the team. It was slow, but it was there. They were no longer flinching when he suggested he might have a new idea. They were listening and asking questions – and not just of him, but of each other. They were looking at the business and wondering what could be better. Mark could see that they were engaged and questioning.

Tonight, Mark was playing chess with John. He hadn't been up for a while. The new house was a few suburbs away, so it wasn't the stroll up the hill it had once been, and settling in to their new home had taken patience. But Mark had watched chess videos online all week, and hoped to surprise his friend and mentor with a good challenge. He was quietly confident.

Mark sat across the board from John, a glass of red wine in hand and a bacon sandwich on the small table beside his chair. The wine was great, and the sandwich was exceptional, but it didn't change the facts on the board in front of him.

Mark had tried one of the gambits the video had said couldn't fail, had tricked Grand Masters, and been called without irony "a sure win." They were barely through the opening, and already Mark was on the run.

John leaned back in his chair and picked up his wine. "I think that's mate in three?" Mark looked around the board, trying to find John's line. There it was, obvious now that he knew it was there. Mark sighed as he knocked over his king.

"Nice work. Well, at least the business is going better than my chess." Mark smiled, thinking that it was easier to lose on the board when the business was winning. He'd hoped to talk about work a little with John.

"That's great news, Mark. I had been wondering how it was going." John was smiling gently. "You've been quiet about it lately, and I didn't want to pry. What's changed?"

Mark thought about it for a moment. "Well, in some ways, nothing major has changed, just a few small changes, ideas shared, and lessons learned. But, somehow, this has had a major impact on the business. The team are happier, clients are ordering more, and we seem to be going from strength to strength."

"I remember your team being a bit reluctant."

"You're right. But after the first change, the leadership meetings went so well that the team seemed much more open to my ideas. They even started to bring ideas of their own to the table. It's been transformational." Mark stopped, surprised at what he had just said. *Transformational* was a big word.

He carried on. "In the last six months, we have made a handful of small changes. First, there were the meetings. Then we read a small book, *The New One Minute Manager*."

"Great book," said John, gesturing for Mark to continue while he began to reset the board.

"After that, we listened to a podcast about decision-making, shared an article about *second-order consequences* and watched a video about economic decision making. After we came across each of these ideas, they became a part of how we talked to each other, a shorthand we all shared. I knew it started having an impact when I started hearing the ideas shared and used by the wider team. They became a part of who we are as an organization, not just something to sit on the shelf in the board room.

"We did try a couple of things that didn't work. One was the Cynefin framework. The team found it interesting, but I don't think they connected with it. They couldn't see how they could use it day to day. It didn't feel like a failure, though. It became more of a step along the way that was interesting, but it didn't become a part of the business. We moved on to something else, and didn't feel like a big deal. It felt natural to let it go and move on." Mark sat back in his chair, taking a moment to reflect.

John finished resetting the board. "One more game?"

"Why not."

BEACH TIME

Mark and Patty walked arm in arm along the beach. Luke was running ahead after Baxter, who was chasing seagulls into the water. They had driven to the beach that morning, and would drive back to their house on the hill in time for lunch with Patricia's mom.

It had been three years since they had sold their dream house by the beach. They had made it through one of the toughest periods of their lives. Mark was ever thankful to Patricia for her understanding.

The business was going from strength to strength. That first small change to the weekly management meeting had been the start of getting the business back on its feet. It hadn't happened overnight, and it had been slow and, at times, unreasonably tough. But now, everything seemed so much easier than it was.

The business was almost unrecognizable. What Mark found really fascinating was that he couldn't put his finger on any one change that had made the difference. There was no silver bullet. Instead, each small change added to the one before to improve the business. Each grain of sand added up until they had a pile, or a heap, or a beach.

They had certainly made some mistakes along the way, but mostly these mistakes had felt like moments of learning. Mark remembered the times he had fallen back into old habits and tried to launch an amazing idea or make big changes without the team's support. But now, it was as if the business had a healthy immune system that would reject such changes quickly and with certainty.

"I've been thinking," Mark started.

"Uh oh," said Patty, laughing.

"About the business. I've been working through what has changed. Why are the changes we are making now easier, more frequent, and more impactful? I was hoping I could tell you about it and see if it makes sense to you?"

"Sure. You've got five minutes before we turn back towards the car."

"Got it – make it snappy." Mark took a deep breath. "I think there are three things that are crucial to making change successful. If I pay attention to each of them the change seems easy. If I miss one, the change seems to stall or fail. When I am thinking about these three things, they are more than attributes or tick boxes. I'm thinking of them as mindsets.

"Firstly, the team has to be working in a space where it is ok to try and fail. I call this one *Safety*.

"Secondly, the team needs to understand the idea well enough to work with it. I'm calling this *Accessibility*.

"Third and last, the team needs to be questioning and wondering, *What could make the business, project, relationship better?* I'm calling this *Curiosity*.

"So what do you think? Imagine it like a Venn diagram. I know you love a good Venn diagram"

Mark looked over to Patty nervously; she took his hand as they walked.

"I can see you have put a lot of thought into this," she said. "Thinking about the changes that you and your team have made, I can see the mindsets clearly in the changes that worked; it makes sense, knowing how you applied them to make the changes happen. Also it seems like the mindsets have changed the types of changes you're making – like they are smaller than they were before. Less... extravagant. And it looks like the whole team is engaged with them. You should be very proud."

Mark beamed.

"I think you have missed something though," she continued. Mark's smile faltered.

"I'm wondering if there's something that sits underneath those three mindsets. An idea that really holds it together. I mean, you've got to have empathy to make all that work."

Mark laughed loudly. "Empathy! I'm not sure how. You remember when that leadership consultant took us through that strengths test? Empathy was ranked about as low as it could get. Definitely not my forte."

It was Patty's turn to laugh. "Yes, I remember. But I think you might have changed. Don't you?"

Mark went quiet. They had reached the end of the beach. They turned and walked back, holding hands towards Luke and Baxter who were fighting for ownership of a large piece of seaweed.

THE WEEKLY MEETING

Mark looked around the table. Amy was looking relaxed as she talked the team through the financials. Carlos was making notes on his playbook. Tyler and Jane had moved to new companies where they were leading management teams of their own. In their place were a couple of new hires: Catherine, who came from a large corporate at the other end of town and whose empathy and warmth were an asset when it came to building relationships with clients and the team; and Padme, who replaced Jane, and whose care and attention really took the role in a different direction.

Ryan had earned his seat at the table, having joined the leadership team six months after that fateful call from Rick. He was a great addition to the team, and his insight and passion for the business had become a huge driver in their success. Beside Ryan sat Mandy, who had been hired to replace Ryan as Mark's PA. She had quickly demonstrated the people skills required for her to take on the role of Head of HR too.

Amy was finishing her explanation of the financials. "Last quarter was good. We made a solid 17 percent profit. This quarter we are on track for around the same. We have robust forecasts for orders for the next 12 months. And we no longer have any customers who account for more than 30 percent of our revenue."

The team let out small congratulatory whoops and cheers. They had come a long way.

"Thank you for your energy and dedication everyone," said

Mark. "You have each contributed to us getting to this point but, most importantly, we have worked as a team. I know that we like to push ahead, but today let's take time to look back and reflect on the changes we've made. Where have we got to?" Mark looked around the room.

Amy leaned forward in her chair. "Well, Mark, it's just like I said it would be. It's unicorns flying over rainbows pooping gold!"

PART II: THE MODEL

GOOD SMALL CHANGE

Making change happen in organizations is hard. There is so much that we want to achieve, and so many obstacles to overcome. And while there are plenty of books out there that will help you with change management, this isn't one of them.

This book is about making progress, however small, and bringing the people of your organization along on the journey with you. It's about creating the right conditions, and then learning to accept the outcome as part of a journey of growth.

Over the years of running a business and watching friends in their businesses, I have noticed a number of things. The first is that there are plenty of ideas out there on how to run, improve and grow your business. There is no shortage of ideas. Many of them are excellent and worthwhile. But secondly, change is hard. To get the ideas from a book, or workshop, or conference session – then apply them – is a challenge for any leader.

This is what *Unicorns Over Rainbows* overcomes. Made within the right workplace culture, small, incremental changes are better than promises of transformational overhauls.

When I sat down to write this book, I thought about how much my business, Boost, had changed since we first started. We've been in operation for over two decades, and the last five years in particular have seen us make some incredible changes. I wondered if what I had done would be useful and helpful to share with other business owners and leaders.

So my team and I wrote a list of all the ideas, methods and mindsets we have created or encountered and successfully woven into the business. We came up with a clear list of 40 items. But looking at that list, it was clear that we hadn't invented anything ourselves! I thought, *All we've done is implement other people's ideas. There's nothing useful to share and no way to help others who have found themselves in similar situations!*

But then it dawned on me. It wasn't about the tools or techniques we had implemented; it was the way that we had managed to move the business forward substantially with these new ideas, while not disrupting the work or the culture.

As we worked through the list of changes we'd made as a team, we were struck by three things:

1. The vast majority of the changes that had made meaningful impacts were not processes or procedures, but mindsets or thinking tools.
2. We struggled to point to one of the 40 or so changes that we had thought of ourselves. Each idea had, inevitably, come from a book, a coach, or another organization.
3. The most impactful changes had come from simple, small ideas. Ideas so simple that it would have been easy to dismiss them as trivial.

Our challenge was to create a simple framework that could help other leaders and organizations make small, meaningful changes too. Over many sessions, we outlined how those key changes had been introduced, we looked at the behaviors and attitudes that had led to successful, meaningful changes, and we eventually came up with the Good Small Change framework.

You could probably guess that the story of Mark's journey to understand change is, in part, my story. What took Mark months took me years. The journey wasn't one of constant progress but rather one step forward, two steps back (into the overdraft usually!). For those who have joined me on this journey, Mark's story will feel very familiar. Rest assured that nothing in Mark's story happened quite the way it's written, and luckily for us, we never had a Jane. I have tried to capture the feelings and create caricatures of the situations to bring the story to life. But what is true is that today we have a great culture, a focused and committed team, and a clear idea of where we are heading. Everyone who has been a part of Boost has contributed to where we are now, and I am thankful for their help and input.

If you come into the office today, you might just see the culture and think that we've done it all in one go. But really, the current culture is the culmination of those 40-plus small changes over the course of the last five years. That's one thing done differently, on average, every six weeks. Our success is more like a Lego creation than a wood carving. We've slowly tried new things, added, and taken away, mixed up pieces, lost a few, and, one experiment at a time, built an exciting workplace that does cool stuff with and for good people.

That means there have been plenty of opportunities for us to try, and to learn. That's what this book is about.

BIG CHANGE CAN WORK

At the heart of the Good Small Change framework is the idea that we should focus on small incremental changes.

Large, sweeping changes work too. But my experience has been that the big changes are hard, disruptive, and very, very expensive. Anyone who is in change management knows this. To eliminate those risks, we can use an approach that instead gets people on board with small steps and the quiet evolution that can be tested and analyzed with each change.

Change itself is never easy – as we saw in Mark's experience – but this most often comes down to the way that we are approaching it. We try to get from point A to point B in one go. We've got our end state in mind, and we want to completely re-architect the way we do business, or the way we approach something.

We want all the imagined results and benefits to be delivered at once. No-one wants to hear that true change happens over a long while – that's nowhere near as dramatic, nor as sexy. But I'm here to tell you that small change works. It continues to work for me, and I hope it might work for you. If it doesn't, that's fine. This isn't the book for you. You're lucky! You can stop reading now and get an hour of your life back. And if you've skipped to Part II and haven't already read the fable, you get three hours of your life back!

I would recommend reading the fable though, because I'm sure you will be able to see yourself and people you have worked with strewn throughout. I was laughing when I wrote it, and I hope you will find it funny too. (I was voted second funniest of my college friends, so that's the only qualification needed, right?)

If, after that, you're still set on big change and all it holds, then I've included some books and resources in the appendix that I think are helpful.

NOW FOR A SECRET

Gather round. This is just for us – those of us who want to try Good Small Change.

The secret is… that trying a good, small change *is* a small change. Try it, and if it works, great! You have another tool in your toolbox. Huzzah!

If it doesn't work for you – also great! You have just spent a small amount of time discovering something that doesn't work, and now you can use that to move forward. Your business and personal life are still intact. You can carry on. If you have the time, send me an email to let me know why it didn't work – I would love to know.

This is why the Good Small Change framework has so much value: It is an agile testing ground for your organization's improvement. At its heart, the Good Small Change model is about incremental cultural change – and three conditions that, when present, enable an organization – or an individual – to make changes that stick. All you need to do is get the basics right.

THE GOOD SMALL CHANGE MODEL

There are three parts to the model – the three mindsets we need to adopt to make good, small, changes.

The first mindset is **Curiosity** – the mindset that drives the change and provides the motivation that keeps us going.

The second is **Accessibility** – the mindset that helps to spread the change throughout our organization.

The third mindset is **Safety** – the mindset that gives us permission to try and fail, and that turns failure into learning.

Let's take a look at these mindsets.

CURIOSITY DRIVES THE CHANGE

Curiosity often leads us to the discovery of a framework, tool, or idea that we think could improve our organization. Curiosity can also lead us to ask questions like, *Could this be better? Why isn't this working?* and *What if?* This might send us looking for answers, or it might prompt us to pull a tool from the bottom of our toolbox – one we were given at a conference, or at a meeting with a friend, or that we read in a book. At the time, we couldn't see a use for that tool, so we threw it into the toolbox. But now we're wondering, *Could this tool be the right thing to help me here?*

Curiosity asks, *What if I didn't stop too long to think about whether this is the right tool but just grabbed it and tried it? What might I learn?*

ACCESSIBILITY SPREADS THE CHANGE

Accessibility makes an idea easy to understand and integrate, so that your team (or even you) can make it happen.

Those working with us need to be able to access the framework, tool, or idea if they are to implement it. To go back to our toolbox analogy, we have to ask, *Is the toolbox locked? Is it on a high shelf at the back of the shed?* If we can't access the tool, we can't share the tool. If we can't access it, we can't use it. But when it's within reach, and in a good condition, then we can put that tool into action. It really is that simple.

SAFETY EMBEDS THE CHANGE

We can't try and fail if it means hurting ourselves or our organization. This is why safety is non-negotiable, and safety as a trait needs to be part of your culture. Our teams won't commit to a change if we don't create, nurture, and maintain a safe environment. Changes need to be safe to fail, not fail-safe.

The smaller the change, the faster we can fail, the smaller the impact of that failure, and the more the failure looks and feels like learning. A small win, however, puts us further ahead. If we don't have a safe environment, then we can't take the failure and hold it up to the light, examine it carefully and work out why it failed and what we might try next. This is why good, small changes are often easier than massive transformations – because it's OK to fail on a small change, but failing on a big transformation can be costly.

When we are working in the shed, we accept that our tools may fail. We take precautions (we wear safety goggles, we push wood through the saw with a stick) so that when the tool or our processes fail, we are still safe. We can still make mistakes, but the costs are much smaller. We're unlikely to lose a finger.

Let's look at each mindset in more detail and see what they mean for you.

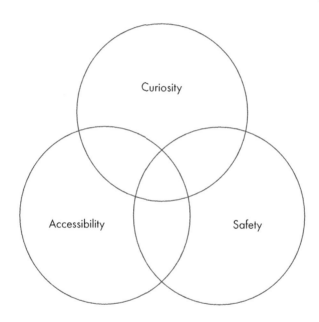

MINDSET I: CURIOSITY

If Mark naturally embodied any of the Good Small Change mindsets, then it's Curiosity.

Curiosity means being open to the world around us and interested in new ideas. Curious people are open and active lifelong learners; they actively pursue new ideas and a deeper understanding of the challenges they face so that they can see how they might solve or improve them.

Curiosity is also one of the most important elements we need in organizations, because it opens the door to doing things differently – and the pursuit of better ways of working.

We joined Mark at a moment of crisis, and we saw that the first thing he jumped to was finding a solution to the immediate problem of sales. He leaned into his natural curiosity – he read the book on flywheels and cannons and snowballs. He talked with John, his informal mentor (and dog walker). His curiosity kept his mind open, and later had him consider what larger systemic problems might have led to the crisis he faced. I hope you're as enthusiastic about finding solutions as Mark!

But a curious leader alone is not enough to drive change through an organization. In order to get others to join this journey of change, we have to find a way to invoke our team's curiosity too – and establish it as a mindset.

At the start, Mark was very much an ideas generator and not much of an ideas follow-througher. He could see new ideas, but didn't stick with any of them long enough to bring them to fruition. He didn't get the engagement of the team – and it took him quite a while to work out how to invoke their mindset of Curiosity.

Without a culture that embraces Curiosity as a mindset, Mark is merely pushing his ideas onto his team and ultimately giving them more things that he wants them to do. This was the case with the business book – a well-meaning gift, which was full of big ideas to implement. But the team didn't have any interest in reading it; it wasn't something they saw as relevant to their work. As Amy said, "I didn't think it was that important."

Later, when introduced to the CRM initiative, Mark's team were more curious. That project didn't see huge successes, even if we were seeing the first signs of the Curiosity mindset (and we'll see why soon). How Mark succeeded in part with the CRM was by introducing its importance for learning about their customer – and how it would make things better for them.

Remember, when people are curious, they're engaged with ideas and interested to learn more about them. We are all more receptive to ideas we've asked about (pull) than ones someone has just told us about (push). You can tell someone what to do all day long, but it's not until they ask something, and actively take an interest, that change happens.

Once the team were curious, they started to commit to the changes.

WHY CURIOSITY DRIVES CHANGE

Once we have become curious, we want to see the outcome, whatever it looks like. We naturally don't like to leave a question unanswered.

Without Curiosity, organizations often stagnate, struggling to change to meet the shifting needs of the market and their people. This was clear with Mark's team: They'd relied too much on the work coming in from Rick, and were quite happy continuing things as they were. There was no drive for doing things better.

The nice thing about Curiosity is that it is, mostly, not threatening. It's the *What if?* It doesn't expect outcomes (other than learning, that is). There is room to move and change, to explore, to hold ideas up, and to share and examine them.

Curiosity doesn't lock us into one course of action. Rather than jumping straight into plans or solutions, we have given ourselves the license to wonder. And that's a powerful thing to have.

This is how Curiosity drives change; it gives us permission to ask ourselves if our products, our processes, or we ourselves could be better. When we are open to these questions, amazing things happen.

CREATING A CULTURE OF CURIOSITY

Innovation has been the catch cry of many organizations for decades. Innovation is incentivized, and innovation teams, awards and even departments are set up. The results often seem to be disappointing given the effort that gets applied. I don't think that innovation is bad, but I think it's hard, and perhaps misunderstood too.

Where innovation is a lagging measure, showing you results after the fact, the Curiosity mindset is a leading measure. Curiosity does a better job at covering the actions that contribute to an innovative or creative outcome. If you're actively curious, innovations will occur; if you're only measuring innovation, it's too late to change what you were doing to get there.

There are many ways to increase your team's Curiosity mindset. Here are some approaches that have worked well for me:

Paint a picture of the future if the change worked

Ask the team to think about what it would look like, what it would feel like. Is it a future that they want to see? Frame up the possibilities for your team and capture the excitement of what it could look like if you implemented this idea and it worked.

Invite individual team members to imagine their place in that future

If this change was alive and working in your business, what would it look like? What part did they play? How does it benefit them? How could the change be good for them and for the team? What contribution does your team make in getting this change off the ground?

Make the change small

The smaller the change, the quicker we see the results. This creates positive reinforcement that makes us crave the next change – because we see the impact that our changes have made.

Ensure that all team members are aligned

Every person on the team has to be aiming for the same target. If you're seeing a problem, make sure others are too. If someone is seeing a problem and others aren't, there's likely a different problem – so get curious and find common ground before you move forward. It is essential to avoid artificial harmony. Do the work to get everyone onto the same page.

Share stories

Your organization is already full of examples of when similar changes were made – use these as 'case studies' of when this type of change worked well and show your team that change is already part of the process.

Remember you are not trying to sell them the idea

You are selling them an answer to a question. You often don't know whether the change is going to work, but you are curious to find out. Your job is to help your team become curious too.

Look at the composition of your team

Using a strengths finder tool like The Table Group's *Working Geniuses* can help find the right people in your organization to support change. Having people on the team that have the full range of working geniuses can be a game changer for affecting change. For Curiosity, you are looking for team members whose zones of genius include qualities like wondering, or the ability to consider the greater potential of a situation (*Wonder* in The Working Genius model). Not all of your team has to have *Wonder* as a working genius but having one or two certainly helps. *Invention* is also useful at this stage, for generating potential experiments and changes that could answer the questions being asked.

YOUR ROLE AS LEADER

As a leader in your organization, your role is clear. You are responsible for creating the conditions for change. It is easy to assume that it is confidence and charisma that drives organizations forward, but it's not. As a leader with a surprising lack of charisma myself, I have had to find other, better ways of getting my team on board. Not only that, but when I rely less on my small amounts of charisma to drive change and focus on the Good Small Change mindsets, I get faster, better, and more consistent results.

Your role is to paint the pictures and tell the stories that have your team asking *What if?* It's to ensure there is enough space for others to start to imagine a different future no matter how big or small. We must model Curiosity for our teams, and let our behavior inspire and teach.

In our fable, we see the team really start to imagine a different future once Mark starts to paint the picture. Mark asks Amy what the future would be like if they achieved their goal of being able to make small, incremental changes in a safe environment. Amy's answer was certainly not what Mark expected, but it was a vivid and powerful image that stuck with Mark, Amy, and the team.

I hope that you are now asking yourself the question, *Could Curiosity work for us?*

MINDSET II: ACCESSIBILITY

Everything seemed so clear to Mark. Time and again he struggled to understand why his team weren't jumping on his ideas. The team didn't know what the change was that Mark actually wanted. They couldn't understand what was needed. Sometimes it was too complex, other times Mark failed to explain or gave no context for the change.

Mark had failed to make his ideas accessible to his team.

Let me lean on the toolbox analogy again. You may understand how to use a bandsaw, but that doesn't ensure that you can use it to cut a piece of wood well. You need to be able to access both the knowledge of *how to use* the bandsaw *and how it works*. The better you know how it works, the better you will be able to use it to its fullest – and use it safely, too.

Accessibility as a mindset involves making an idea or concept available for the people who need to know it. When ideas are accessible, your people can connect with how an idea can impact them and make their lives better. It's not just about describing an idea – it's about showcasing the impact it can and will have, and then leading your people to it. We can't define the Accessibility of an idea by the amount of work we put into sharing information – only by the recipient's ability to access the information that we share.

Mark failed to make his key ideas accessible until very late in the game – and this prevented his team from connecting meaningfully with the impact they could create and how it might benefit them. With the book, Mark was excited about what he'd read, and assumed his senior leadership team would be too. But because he didn't make any efforts to showcase the ideas within, or paint a picture of how they could implement any of the learnings, he didn't connect his team with what the book was for. With the CRM, he put in no real effort to make sense of it with his team. It wasn't just that it looked confusing – it was unclear not only how to navigate the concept, but also why they should follow the processes. The result was plenty of that familiar nodding and smiling – but no accountability, and no action! He'd inspired some curiosity by connecting the CRM to the outcome of making gains in the sales, but without the mindset of Accessibility, it was too far removed to be meaningful.

We each have different speeds at which we take on new knowledge. And we all have limits on how much we can learn at a time. We're all starting from a different place, with different life experiences and prior learning to draw on. The chances are that, if you're reading this book, then you are one of the lucky ones who finds acquiring and integrating new knowledge easy and enjoyable. Take the time to ensure that your team truly understands the concepts, the processes, and why this change is important. These are the foundations that the change is built on.

An important note: It's not that we want the change to happen slowly. There is just a good chance that *you* need to slow down. You are a team running this race; be there to pick others up if they stumble. You need to cross the finish line together.

HOW ACCESSIBILITY SPREADS CHANGE

When you create a culture of Accessibility, you empower your team to embrace and challenge ideas.

Nothing makes me happier than when I overhear a team member explaining a concept or tool that we have introduced to the organization to someone else. Especially if it's me that they are explaining it to! When we make changes to the way we work, they are usually introduced to one smaller team first. If the change works, the team is often so enthusiastic about it that they become the evangelists for this change in the organization. As each team sees success with the change, they also become evangelists. Eventually one day it has become a part of 'the way we work.'

In order for this organic growth to happen, the change has to be accessible. Often the way we've communicated, shared, and fostered the change becomes the model for others when spreading the change more widely. Change is therefore dependent on how accessible we made it initially.

Make the change easy to access and, if it's a good change, it will naturally spread throughout the organization.

HOW DO I MAKE CHANGE ACCESSIBLE?

Pick people up at their bus stop

Everyone that you interact with has their own life history, mental state, experience, assumptions, prior knowledge, and so on. So it pays to meet them where they're at – their individual 'bus stop' – not where you want them to be! Adjust what and how you teach to suit the people you're dealing with and their needs, situation, and current knowledge. You're driving the bus – but you need to meet them at their stop.

Draw on your team's existing knowledge

Picking up a new idea takes brainpower. But you can reduce the cognitive load of a new idea by taking advantage of your team's current understanding. Show that the new idea is related to or linked with an existing concept – that it's not entirely unlike what you're already doing or an idea you've already seen in practice – and the new concept will be only a short step rather than a big leap.

Tell stories that illustrate where a similar change is already working

Like with Curiosity, stories help us understand that change doesn't have to be scary or big – because you're often already doing it. Use examples and stories to show your team that!

Ask each team member to give an example from their life where they have seen this change work (or not)

If your team can name an example of where a similar change has had a positive impact, then they'll prove to themselves that this idea can and does work. If they have an example of the idea not working, then together you can find out why – and use this for your own journey.

Keep it small

Big changes are often scarier than smaller ones, because there's a lot more at risk with a "transformation" than an evolution. Build up to bigger change by putting it together one piece at a time. Remember I said that my company was more like a Lego creation than a wood carving!

Think about tools that simplify the change

Checklists and playbooks make processes much easier to follow – especially if you're starting out and there's a new set of steps to adhere to. Knowing that you can move from Step A to Step B will give your team confidence that they're doing it well.

Make it part of your routine

If it's not done regularly or consistently, then it's easy for a good, small change to get left behind. By making it part of your day-to-day (or week-to-week) processes and routines, you reinforce its importance – and get to really see whether it's going to be successful or not.

Make it part of your business's vocabulary

Your workplace already has its own internal language, jargon and specific terms that mean nothing to anyone outside your group. (I've thought that a good business culture is a bit like a cult in this way!) These shorthand terms help you and your team recall wider concepts easily – as well as being a way of helping you create a unique touchpoint that aligns with your organization's values. For example, if we want to have a conversation with a colleague or as a team about something delicate but important, we might ask to have a 'crucial.' We'll all know what it means, but an outsider would likely have no clue. Once your team starts using a new concept daily as part of your vocabulary, you'll know that it's embedded.

Create a scorecard so that your team know the activities needed to make the change and can track their progress

I generally find KPIs to be too one-dimensional, since they can come at the cost of your wider culture. But when KPIs are associated with a strategic change, they can help keep you on track with your progress towards a goal. So, if you have quarterly goals or 90-day sprints, then tracking progress against both soft goals (around general culture and the 'spirit' of a workplace) and hard goals (sales, targets, numbers) will keep you motivated and make sure everyone's still thinking about the balance of culture and targets too!

Start with Why

Simon Sinek's *Why* approach has helped countless businesses when it comes to purpose, direction, and a bigger picture. If you haven't already watched Sinek's TED Talk or read one of his books, then here's the short version: We tend to make decisions emotionally first, then justify them with logic. The *What* you do – AKA your product or service – isn't why customers come back to you. Instead, if you lead your marketing, sales, and culture with a *Why* – a purpose, cause, or reason to follow your brand – then both your customers and your team are more likely to stick around and won't drift off whenever a newer, shinier product appears. Leading with your *Why* not only helps with getting your audience connected to you (e.g. into your email database), but also gives your team a reason to invest their skills in your organization.

YOUR ROLE AS LEADER

Being able to make ideas accessible – and having a team that shares ideas with greater accessibility – makes change that much easier. When ideas and changes within a business have been made accessible, you see clarity and understanding. There is alignment and action. There's no confusion. Everyone is on the same page and in agreement about what's happening and what you're trying to achieve – as well as how you are going about it. There is commitment – which is what drives results.

You're responsible for making a change accessible. You may not be the one who does all of the work of making the change accessible, but you are responsible for ensuring that everyone on the team understands and can use this knowledge, tool or process.

Some of us are natural teachers; we may easily take on this work and enjoy it. Others are not, and may work with a trainer or coach to make the change accessible. Or another team member with change management experience may step into this role. You don't have to do the work – but you need to ensure that it happens.

Take the time to notice how your team is reacting. Are they finding the information easy to access? Are they quickly drawing parallels to previous experiences? Are they engaged and contributing? These are all good signs that they're able to access the information that is being presented to them.

MINDSET III: SAFETY

Safety has become a catch cry in business, particularly when talking about psychological safety – the idea that we can openly share ideas without fear of blame or ridicule. As leaders, we work hard to make the environment safe for our teams. Not just because it's right that everyone should feel safe, but also because it's an advantage for your organization to have diversity of thought. You benefit when your people are comfortable knowing that they can ask challenging questions.

Safe doesn't mean 'without risk.' There's always going to be an element of risk in business. Instead, your team should be able to make changes without the fear that getting it wrong is going to cost them their jobs or the like; they need to know that they won't be embarrassed, rejected, or punished for sharing. This is Safety as a mindset.

How many meetings have you been in where there truly was this kind of Safety mindset? As a leader are you able to make every situation safe for your team? Can you communicate ideas in a way that your people feel comfortable taking those ideas on board, and that the risks of a new idea don't outweigh the benefits?

Tempting though it is, it's impossible to put guard-rails around everything to make it safer – at least not if you want to also be effective. Too safe, or too comfortable, and nothing ever changes. Too risky, and you could lose everything. When we focus too much on guarding against failure, we risk creating bureaucracy and unnecessary barriers. It risks making it harder to do what we're trying to do. We push too hard and see things fail in new ways, which we then create further rules for, in order to mitigate that failure. And on it goes, until you've got a dysfunctional environment where Safety as a mindset isn't embodied, and it's not possible to do anything. Not to mention that if all we're thinking about is failure, that's what we're heading towards. We need to actively avoid trying to make change initiatives fail-safe.

Many of us have never experienced true Safety as a mindset in our organization, and as a leader, it is all too easy to mistake compliance, harmony, and agreement as this Safety. Mark struggles with this in the fable. Mark's team likes him, they respect him, and they work hard to achieve his goal, but in the background the team is trying to avoid failing. They don't want to see Mark's disappointed face!

With the book, Mark promised that it would change their business and get them back to where they once were. The CRM, he assured them, would "fix everything." Later, despite the team being engaged and curious, and the lessons made accessible, the ideas from the movie Mark shared didn't connect because the team weren't feeling safe enough to try them. The result was that they failed to commit to the meeting agenda – and never tried it long enough or thoroughly enough to see any meaningful results.

Mark is working hard to make the environment safe, but he misses what is truly going on around him. The team doesn't want to disappoint Mark; everything feels so important that failing feels like it could sink the whole business. This is an all-too-common fear in small businesses; in larger businesses it is often an individual's status that is at stake. Safety was not embodied as a mindset.

As leaders, we unconsciously create expectations for our teams. It's not just a case of saying to your team, "Hey, don't worry – this is a safe space to experiment." We have to model trying and failing, and more than that, it is our job to ensure that the failure is itself safe.

When you're thinking about trying new things in this way – as collecting learnings for your toolkit – there's more commitment to ideas over the long term. Seeing small wins along the way keeps people going. Each win gives permission for the next, and you build from there. There's a gradual leveling up. A culture of Safety lowers the stakes. It's not big and flashy, but it produces incremental change that's easier to spot only when you look back over a longer time period.

I've always found it helpful to experience something before I try to create or replicate it in a different environment. Chances are that there have been times in your life, whether in an organization or not, that you have felt completely safe in a group situation. Cast your mind back to this time. What did it feel like? How did you behave? What was it that created the Safety? What were you able to achieve in this safe environment?

WHY SAFETY EMBEDS CHANGE

Safety gives us the space to work in. When Safety exists in your organization's culture, there's a commitment to action, and a willingness to try.

A 'culture of Safety' could also be rephrased as a 'culture of learning'. It's a culture that encourages experiments, and as a result, it feels safe and even fun to be innovative. It's an environment where the focus of the outcomes has moved from *needing to win*, to instead be about *wanting to learn*. In fact, there's a general acceptance that, to improve, you have to learn.

What you get is a team of people who are willing to try things – and not just once, but again and again. You have commitment to an idea or potential change. People will try, see what works and what doesn't, and then make tweaks or try again accordingly. And there's not the belief that something needs to work the first time in order to be valid.

Where a culture of Safety exists, there is time built into initiatives to understand the learnings and allow for adjusting the course accordingly. That's why you should be prepared to tolerate a dip into underperformance when you're trying something new, as opposed to quickly jumping to the conclusion that an initiative isn't working. Small changes are safer because they tend to represent smaller, more tolerable dips in performance while your team adjusts to new procedures.

CREATING A CULTURE OF SAFETY

A key to creating and maintaining Safety is attention. Inattention leads to Safety disappearing. Safety takes effort and attention to create and can disappear with one word, look or action. It's Brené Brown's apocryphal jar of marbles: Each time we work to create Safety, another marble goes into the jar. Sometimes we make mistakes and marbles come out of the jar. But if you take the jar off the table, lift it over your head and smash it on the ground before storming out of the room, then it can take a long, long time before you ever have a jar of marbles again. Trust takes time to build, but is easily shattered.

Here are some ways to increase Safety in your teams:

Ask questions; don't offer answers

One of the best things you can do is to help your team discover a solution rather than forcing it on them. So, be patient, give your team time to come to terms with the situation and the opportunity ahead, and explore what answers could look like. Asking questions – and being curious – will make sure that everyone gets the chance to get on solid ground. Don't push to get an outcome. Instead, support your team to find the outcome in their own time. Give them plenty of chances to be heard and have any concerns addressed.

Take on the role of facilitator

Talk tentatively and leave space for others. Leaders are often expected to drive the conversation – but that can also make us drive the conversation in the direction we thought was right before we entered the room! Instead, think of your role as that of a facilitator: Having no dog in the race or commitment to a particular outcome. Instead ensure that everyone has an equal voice, and that everyone is given the chance to speak for roughly the same amount of time. The facilitator also steps away from making any decisions – and lets the room arrive at a conclusion together.

Model trying and failing for your team

In a safe environment, failure isn't just likely – it's expected. Once you embrace failing as part of the process, your team will become much more comfortable trying things out and seeing what happens. The scientific process can be a real help here: Adjust one variable, test it out, and record your results. As a leader, if your team knows that you're on the journey with them, then they're more likely to support a journey of growth together. But that also means owning your mistakes. So when mistakes happen, share them with the team and explore what learnings you can draw.

Share stories of when you have failed, what it felt like and how you recovered from it

If you are going to learn one skill, my suggestion is to learn how to apologize promptly and properly. Vulnerability is a cornerstone of cultures that feel safe. In opening yourself up and sharing stories of failure, you show humility and grace in the face of mistakes. It also helps to apologize early – and often. For extra reading, check out *The One Minute Apology* by Ken Blanchard, a really great book on how to apologize. It's important that apologies and owning your failures aren't the same as telling horror stories. One is a learning experience; the other is meant to scare away your audience, often according to a pre–existing agenda. Learn how to spot the difference in yourself and your team!

Take care of how you show up

A boat can't move through the water without leaving a wake. When you show up, you bring with you your energy, behavior, and attitude – and that can have an impact on the people around you, even when you don't realize it. This isn't a sign to silence negative emotions or downplay concerns! Instead, embody your values authentically, and, if you find yourself struggling, let your peers know. You might even find it opens you up for a helpful and healing conversation with a peer.

Talk about what will happen if the change doesn't work

Being safe to fail means that your team really understands the cost if an idea fails – and it shouldn't be a serious cost when dealing with good, small changes. How will you approach failure as a team? How will you learn together?

Set clear and explicit expectations for everyone on the team – including yourself

We often get upset with someone because they didn't act according to expectations – but if that person had no ideas of what those expectations were, then it's hardly fair to be upset! A culture of accountability sets clear expectations within a team to make sure that you're all on the same page and know the measures by which you're being judged. That includes ourselves – both knowing what our own personal expectations are, and what others expect of us.

Start with something internal

Make the change for yourselves and your own business, behind closed doors, before taking it out to clients. This way you can try again and again until you really get it working, then apply it to a client – and later more clients, always learning from each experiment and discovering better ways. Your team can be confident that the idea is safe and robust and they can share it with your clients without stress.

YOUR ROLE AS LEADER

Of the Good Small Change mindsets, Safety is where you have the biggest part to play as a leader. You are 100% responsible for creating and maintaining high levels of psychological safety within your team, and ensuring that everyone else respects the need for Safety too. That's fundamental for leadership today.

Developing a safe culture starts with taking the time to understand what your team needs in order to be safe – what support they need, and how you create a space that works for everyone. Like all leadership skills, this is an ongoing process. You'll need to take stock regularly of where you and your team are at, and what else is needed to create and maintain Safety as your team grows and changes, as your industry moves forward, and as your collective skills and experience shifts with time.

A note of caution: Accidents happen, and you need to own them. In my journey as a leader, I have worked hard to extinguish the behaviors in me that I felt harmed our Safety culture, like showing frustration, pushing too hard for what I believed was right, or viewing my team as passengers and not co-drivers. Over the years – and trust me it was *years* –

I have become better at avoiding these behaviors. The result has been a marked improvement in the Safety of my teams, and consequently the results in the business. But still, I regularly undermine our Safety. Not on purpose, but through thoughtlessness. The jar of marbles sometimes takes a hit.

When I look back at these situations, I often see that I was trying to do one of two things: Make myself look good, or shift the focus away from myself because I felt exposed or insecure. In the past I would push these situations to the back of my mind and move on with my life. Of course, I would occasionally experience that sudden recollection of the event and feel that involuntary shudder and shame flood through me.

Today I see these mistakes differently.

Firstly, we all make mistakes – and we need to make sure that we and our teams have permission to be imperfect. I hope this section has helped you get comfortable with this idea too.

Secondly, I am often in a position as a business owner where people are less likely to call me out, which means I have to hold myself accountable. As the leader, you'll need to continually work on your skills to build Safety. And you'll need to talk to your teams about Safety and how to get the best work from them. Set their expectations of the environment you're working to create – and ask them to hold you accountable to that safe culture.

Thirdly, every mistake is an opportunity. If I can apologize to the team for my mistake, it becomes a powerful way to work towards re-establishing Safety and modeling the behavior I would like to see. We are all still learning.

BRINGING IT ALL TOGETHER

These three mindsets have to work together. As we've seen throughout Mark's story, you can't just have Curiosity or Accessibility or Safety and ask your team to make good, small changes to evolve your organization.

Any one of these qualities is good to have in an organization. Curiosity means that you're prepared to ask questions about how things operate, and look for new ways of doing things. Accessibility keeps the lines of communication open, and ensures that ideas are relevant to your people. Safety ensures that small changes and challenges are possible, and even expected, as part of your organization's evolution. If you have one of these, then well done – you're on the right path.

But as we've seen, just one of these isn't enough if you want to get your team on board with lasting, meaningful changes.

Only when all three come together do you get results. This was the case for Mark at the end of the story, once he'd engaged the team's curiosity and presented the accessible idea of small changes made safely over time. This was only possible when he'd listened to his people; he'd understood the challenges they faced and approached change with them in mind.

YOUR HIDDEN SUPERPOWER: EMPATHY

When we were putting the model together, we hit a problem. The three mindsets were really working in harmony, and the combination really hit the nail on the head. But we discovered that we had missed a crucial part of the model: Empathy.

Try as we might, we couldn't quite fit it into the model. It wasn't a mindset separate from the others. And it wasn't a concept that could be extracted from the others without it all falling apart. As we began to describe empathy and its importance to the model, however, we realized that it actually underpinned every aspect, and the model as a whole. To quote The Big Lebowski's The Dude, "That rug really tied the room together."

Having the capacity to understand and feel what another person is experiencing, to place oneself in another's position and appreciate their perspective and mental state, can't be neglected. Being aware of your team's emotional states and perspectives, sharing experiences and needs, staying away from judgment, and taking actions to improve and support your people can't be 'nice-to-haves' in any organization. And without empathy, you can't have a culture of Safety, or Curiosity, or Accessibility.

WHY BE MORE EMPATHIC?

Empathetic leaders seem to be strongly underrated and underestimated, often getting crowded out by the hard taskmasters focused on KPIs and profit margins. It's often seen as a weakness rather than a strength. In my experience, when an empathetic team member shares how they are feeling, those feelings are often dismissed or minimized. It is seen as an annoyance or a distraction that others have feelings.

I get it. Feelings really annoyed me for the longest time. They seemed to just get in the way of getting work done. But that's probably because empathy has not been my natural strength. We use Clifton Strengths Finder at Boost to help us work better together and find as many opportunities as possible for team members to work in their strengths. When I got my results, Empathy was ranked 31 out of 34. Not a strong showing. So, when I am talking about empathy, it's from the position of someone for whom it does not naturally arise. I have had to work at it. The empathy is not strong with this one.

But what I've found has completely changed my attitude towards feelings and empathy, and now I find myself digging for the feelings and leaning on my empathetic team members to get a better understanding of situations. I want to know what they're feeling and what perspectives they bring, because no one of us knows everything about what's in front of us – but together our diverse experiences and knowledge bases mean that we can tackle things from different perspectives and land on solutions that any one of us might miss. Plus, research has shown that the ability of empathic leaders to see problems from others' perspectives makes them less self-centered and more flexible in problem solving.

Empathy helps reduce conflict, increases sales and referrals, accelerates innovation, improves engagement, raises your market value, and unifies your team with a supportive culture.

In short, it's just good business.

HOW DO WE USE EMPATHY?

Empathy is generally put into cognitive (intellectual) or emotional camps. Emotional empathy refers to the ability to understand and often reflect another's emotions. Cognitive empathy refers to the ability to understand another's perspective or mental state.

In the context of Good Small Change, empathy helps us understand how the people around us, both those effecting the change and those being affected by it, may be feeling at any time. It helps us consider others' perspectives and what we can do better. Empathy drives us through the model, enabling us to see how the change might be made accessible for the team we are working with. It opens us up to courageous conversations. It can tell us why a person, team or organization may not be curious and what blocks might be getting in the way. And it lets us feel when a culture of Safety is embodied or absent.

Luckily for both of us, empathy seems to be coachable. I've learned to be more empathic and embrace my feelings, and I'm not an outlier here. Neuropsychological studies suggest that, with adequate coaching, people can become more prosocial, altruistic, and compassionate, and that such changes will be visible in brain imaging studies. Considering the business benefits that come with that empathy, you'd probably agree that it's something worth working on!

There is another way to get more empathy in your teams: Hire it. When creating a team, you'll want to build a portfolio of skills and abilities. Empathy and other so-called 'soft' skills are just as important to the strength of your operations as any technical ability. Be on the lookout for team members who might be strongly empathetic, bring them into your team, and ensure that their voices are heard.

DIAGNOSTICS: WHAT MIGHT BE MISSING?

At times it can be difficult to determine why Good Small Change isn't working. Even if you think you've cultivated curiosity, worked hard on creating a safe environment, made ideas accessible by picking people up at their bus stops, and practiced empathy, it might feel as if something isn't quite working.

If you're committed to Good Small Change – and I hope you are – then the simple tool below will help you uncover what's getting in the way. It's unlikely to tell you the whole story, but might just be the thread that you can start pulling to unravel the whole sweater.

Check out the diagram on the following page.

The Good Small Change Model

When something is missing

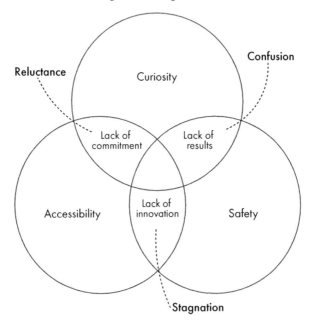

IF YOU'RE SEEING...

CONFUSION, OR A LACK OF RESULTS

If your team is unsure of what is happening or how, or each team member seems to have a different idea of what to do or why, then this often points to a lack of the Accessibility mindset.

But even if the team has committed to the change and are working hard to make it happen, and the results just aren't there, a lack of Accessibility might still be the problem. The team is trying to make a change but aren't fully understanding what is needed or why. So: Can the change be simplified or reduced in scope? Or do you need to spend more time making it accessible? Think about how you can make the idea easier to understand and integrate for your team. Remember, they'll each be at different parts of their journey, so will need different levels and kinds of support.

STAGNATION, OR A LACK OF INNOVATION

Sometimes your team is putting forward similar ideas and approaches, or team members are unable to identify areas that could be improved. Or it feels like *Groundhog Day*, with the same changes enacted time and again, with the same results.

A lack of the Curiosity mindset in your team's culture will mean that they might not see any place for improvement or innovation. They are lacking Curiosity – that spark to ask *What if?*

Remember, Curiosity asks questions and is eager to explore new ideas, just to see where they'll take you. Have you painted a vivid picture of what the future could look like? Is the team regularly exposed to new learning and ideas? How can you encourage and inspire?

RELUCTANCE, OR A LACK OF COMMITMENT

If your teams are reporting that they are overwhelmed, or they're not trying to effect change, then they might be avoiding pain. There might be no sense of follow-through. The team could understand what needs to be done and why, but everything else seems more important or gets in the way. The problem may not be too much work. It may be that the team doesn't feel safe to try. If you never try, you never fail, after all. It's time to have a look at your culture of Safety.

Do you have true Safety, or do you have artificial harmony? Is failure a chance to learn, or does it turn someone into a negative example? Does everyone have a voice and a chance to express their perspective and ideas, and if not, what needs to be addressed?

CONCLUSION: WHERE TO NEXT?

I have described the fact that taking an incremental, small change approach has hugely benefited my business and my team. I haven't talked about the types of changes that we have made or the impact each has had. I hope that pulling the curtain back on this will give you an idea of how this may help your organization. You might even want to try them yourself.

Our changes have varied in size. One was to redefine our attitudes in just eight words, adopting Winston Churchill's aphorism "Never let a good crisis go to waste." This phrase has become a catch cry for us at Boost. It has given us the space and the permission to find opportunity in even the direst of circumstances.

Another was to adopt fundamental thinking tools, such as 'second-order thinking' as explained by Howard Marks in his book *The Most Important Thing* (but that we actually encountered by listening to a podcast as a team). While first-order thinking looks at consequences as either 'good' or 'bad,' second- and third-order thinking asks *And then what?* of the consequences to make sure that we've considered the bigger picture. When we discussed this as a team, we used examples from the recent and not-so-recent past to illustrate and share the idea. Now it's on the tip of our tongues whenever we face a difficult decision. Considering the second (and subsequent) order consequences has enabled us to journey through difficult decisions together and given us the courage to accept negative first-order consequences when we had previously been reluctant.

We wanted to build a culture of Accountability, so we started with what we thought would be an obvious place – a book titled *Crucial Accountability* by Kerry Patterson, Ron Switzler, A Grenny, and Joseph McMillan. But that was only the start. In reading *Crucial Accountability*, we realized that there was an even more important set of skills we needed to acquire first: Crucial conversations. So, we brought in a trainer, and over two days, we dove into the crucial conversation element. This included – and please brace yourself for the horror – roleplay. I'm pleased to report that we all survived. And the tools and skills of crucial conversation are now a cornerstone of our culture of feedback and accountability. We have even created a crucial conversation planner that guides us through these conversations as needed.

We built a list. Every tool, idea, maxim, book, and framework we use to run the business is on that list. This list has grown to around 50 items now, and they've all added to our daily vocabulary. They're not tools rusting in the back of the shed, dusty and forgotten. They're living and breathing at every level of our organization, and a sign of how much we've evolved – and continue to evolve – on our journey.

Is that what you want for your organization?

IS THIS A BOOK ABOUT CHANGE MANAGEMENT?

And is Good Small Change actually just a change management framework?

Great questions – and ones I'm glad that you asked. I don't think of Good Small Change, or this book, in that way. The Good Small Change model enables us to set the starting conditions of change, and then accept the results we get – great or not-so-great – as part of the journey towards our goals.

Let me try and illustrate this with an analogy. For a while, I was learning to fly small aircraft. It was great fun, and a really exciting challenge. One day early in my training, I was in the plane with my instructor. He was explaining how we use the throttle in the aircraft like this:

In a plane, we set the throttle, and we accept the performance – that is, the climb rate, airspeed etc. We then use the controls to maintain that performance, constantly adjusting the throttle and steering to achieve and sustain that performance. As the conditions change, so does your response. And yes, sometimes, you're going to hit turbulence.

This is the difference I see between change management and Good Small Change. With change management, we set the outcome we want and constantly adjust to achieve that outcome – we are managing the change itself. But with Good Small Change, we set the conditions and accept the outcomes; we don't track its implementation or our progress against an outcome other than trial and error. Often we have no idea what the result will be. But the change is small, and consequently, it's reversible. If it's working, great! If it's not, then let's try something else.

Imagine what this success could look like in your organization.

What can we expect to get from adopting the Good Small Change model? Our goal is incremental, sustainable change. That's it.

The Good Small Change Model
The goal

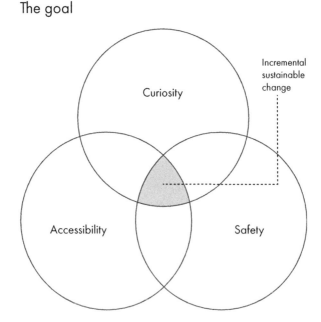

We have looked at the three mindsets. Curiosity drives change and provides the motivation that keeps us going. Accessibility helps to spread the change throughout our organization. Safety allows us to try and fail, which turns failure into learning.

We have also looked at the hidden superpower that underpins the model: Empathy. And we know what we are trying to achieve: Incremental, sustainable change.

Once you have encountered the model, none of this should come as a surprise. The Good Small Change model is simple to understand and easy to apply. I hope that when you look at this model, you say to yourself, "Obviously, I need those things to make change happen."

When I look back at the last decade to see which ideas or tools have had the most impact on my business, the team and myself, they inevitably have one thing in common: They are simple. Simple is often overlooked. Sometimes we look for novel, complex, or sophisticated answers – ideas we haven't encountered before, or that have a steep learning curve. They may seem extra valuable because it feels like we have learnt something new or opened the door to an exciting new world. But simple can be the most powerful.

Simple to understand doesn't always mean simple to achieve, of course. This is certainly the case in the Good Small Change model. When I think about Safety, it is immediately apparent that changes will wither on the vine without it. But, even now, I can find myself in the middle of a conversation, wondering how I just managed to destroy the Safety I had spent all week building. Or I can be so passionate and excited about a new idea that I steamroll through the team, leaving them flattened behind me.

Every change that we introduce lives and dies on how much attention we have paid to the three mindsets. Sometimes we are so excited that we race ahead of the team. We leave them behind, wondering what we are talking about and why it's important, and they feel unseen and confused.

I have become more consistent in applying the Good Small Change model within my business. As a result, I have seen a real change in my team. Where once they were confused and reluctant, now they are engaged and eager. This is what I want to share with you.

Good Small Change is simple, but its impact has been profound for me. I hope it will be for you too.

REFERENCES AND FURTHER READING

I've drawn on a lot of reading and the thinking of others to create this book. Here are few that deserve special mention.

Simon Sinek introduced the concepts of *Start with Why* and *The Golden Circle* to a wide audience in his 2009 TED Talk, and through his first book (*Start with Why*, also released in 2009).

I refer to *The 6 Types of Working Genius* (Matt Holt, 2022) in the section on 'Creating a culture of Curiosity.' It's another brainchild of Patrick Lencioni, who gave us *The Five Dysfunctions of a Team* (Jossey-Bass, 2002). This new model gives us six zones of genius that a team member might have, including *Wonder, Invention, Discernment, Galvanizing, Enablement and Tenacity* (WIDGET).

In this model, *The Genius of Wonder* is "The natural gift of pondering the possibility of greater potential and opportunity in each situation. The Gift of Invention, meanwhile, is "The natural gift of creating original and novel ideas and solutions." Both will be valuable in your team, especially if you need to boost Curiosity.

Tomas Chamorro-Premuzic argues that empathic leaders are less self-centered and more flexible at problem solving. Check out *Why Do So Many Incompetent Men Become Leaders?: (And How to Fix It)* (Harvard Business Review Press, 2019). It's a great read for demystifying how and why we tend to equate leadership potential with destructive personality traits – and what we can do about it.

Empathy can be developed – and its impact in the brain shows in neural imaging. If you're keen to learn more, check out Tammi R. A. Kral et al., "Neural Correlates of Video Game Empathy Training in Adolescents: A Randomized Trial," *NPJ Science of Learning 3*, no. 13 (2018).

Below is a non-comprehensive list of recommended reads:

By Patrick Lencioni (and others)
The Five Temptations of a CEO (Jossey-Bass, 1998)
The Four Obsessions of an Extraordinary Executive (Jossey-Bass, 2000)
The Five Dysfunctions of a Team (Jossey-Bass, 2002)
Death by Meeting (Jossey-Bass, 2004)
Silos, Politics and Turf Wars (Jossey-Bass, 2006)
The Truth About Employee Engagement (Jossey Bass, 2007)
The 3 Big Questions for a Frantic Family (Jossey-Bass, 2007)
Getting Naked (Jossey-Bass, 2010)
The Advantage (Jossey-Bass, 2012)
The Ideal Team Player (Jossey-Bass, 2016)
The Motive (Jossey-Bass, 2020)
The 6 Types of Working Genius (Matt Holt, 2022)

By Jim Collins (and others)
Good to Great (Penguin, 2001)
Built to Last (Penguin, 2005)
Great by Choice (Penguin, 2011)
Beyond Entrepreneurship 2.0 (Penguin, 2020)

By Ken Blanchard (and others)
The One Minute Apology (HarperCollins, 2003)
Helping People Win at Work (FT Press, 2009)
Leadership and the One Minute Manager (HarperCollins, 2013)
The New One Minute Manager (HarperCollins, 2015)

Who: The A Method for Hiring by Geoff Smart and Randy Street (Random House, 2008)

Fierce Conversations by Susan Scott (Little, Brown, 2004)

Uncommon Service by Frances Frei and Anne Morriss (Harvard Business Review Press, 2012)

Blue Ocean Strategy by W. Chan Kim and Renée A. Mauborgne (Pan Macmillan UK, 2017)

Small Giants: Companies That Choose to Be Great Instead of Big by Bo Burlingham (Portfolio, 2007)

Simple Numbers, Straight Talk, Big Profits! by Greg Crabtree (Greenleaf Book Group, 2011)

Daring Greatly by Brené Brown (Penguin, 2013)

Crucial Conversations by Kerry Patterson, Joseph Grenny, Ron McMillan and Al Switzler (McGraw-Hill, 2012)

Crucial Accountability by Kerry Patterson, Joseph Grenny, Ron McMillan, Al Switzler and David Maxfield (McGraw-Hill, 2013)

Be the Hero by Noah Blumenthal (ReadHowYouWant.com, 2010)

Chief Joy Officer by Richard Sheridan (Penguin, 2018)

The Great Game of Business by Jack Stack and Bo Burlingham (Profile Books, 2013)

Hyper Sales Growth by Jack Daly (Advantage, 2014)

Mindset: How You Can Fulfil Your Potential by Carol Dweck (Little, Brown, 2012)

The Power of Habit by Charles Duhigg (Random House, 2012)

The Principles of Product Development Flow by Don Reinertsen (Celeritas, 2009)

Scaling Up (Rockefeller Habits 2.0) by Verne Harnish (Gazelles Incorporated, 2014)

The Checklist Manifesto by Atul Gawande (Profile, 2010)

The War of Art by Steven Pressfield (Black Irish Entertainment, 2002)

The L Factor: 8 Ways for Cultivating Young Leaders by Chonya Johnson (derf Consults, 2012)

Multipliers: How the Best Leaders Make Everyone Smarter by Liz Wiseman (HarperCollins, 2010)

Out of Our Minds: Learning to be Creative by Ken Robinson (Wiley, 2001)

The Power of Now by Eckhart Tolle (New World Library, 1999)

Drive: The Surprising Truth About What Motivates Us by Dan Pink (Canongate Books, 2010)

The Likeability Factor by Tim Sanders (Harmony/Rodale, 2005)

FIND OUT MORE

Some of you will be wanting to know more about those "40 small changes" that I've made over the last five years to improve my business. You can learn about what made those good small changes successful over on my website.

Head to **nathandonaldson.com/unicornsoverrainbows**

ACKNOWLEDGEMENTS

There have been so many people that have helped me on this project.

Sarah and Elliot thank you so much for your endless support and patience throughout.

Christina and Dave at Intelligent Ink – your encouragement and enthusiasm gave me the motivation I needed to get this to the finish line. I appreciate your collaborative approach and that you kept pushing me to improve.

Lester, Tim, Ryan, Tom, David, Rebecca, Tiana, Jeongeel, Sean, Craig, and Richard – thank you for reading the early drafts and providing valuable feedback and suggestions.

Hannah, thank you for the fantastic cover design.

Alex, thanks heaps for the coffee and the typesetting.

Printed in Great Britain
by Amazon